Better Off Out?

Better Off Out?

The benefits or costs of EU membership

Revised edition

BRIAN HINDLEY
MARTIN HOWE

The Institute of Economic Affairs

First published in Great Britain in 1996 by
The Institute of Economic Affairs
2 Lord North Street
Westminster
London SW1P 3LB

This revised edition published in 2001 by
The Institute of Economic Affairs
in association with Profile Books Ltd

A CIP catalogue record for this book is available from the British Library.

ISBN 0 255 36502 0

Many IEA publications are translated into languages other than English or are
reprinted. Permission to translate or to reprint should be sought from the
General Director at the address above.

Typeset in Stone by MacGuru
info@macguru.org.uk

Printed and bound in Great Britain by Hobbs the Printers

CONTENTS

THE AUTHORS

Brian Hindley

Brian Hindley is a consultant on trade-policy matters to a number of international organisations. He is Emeritus Reader in Trade Policy Economics at the London School of Economics, and has also lectured, in the past two years, at SciencesPo in Paris, at LUISS in Rome and at the University of Amsterdam Law School. He is co-chairman of the Bruges Group.

His recent publications include 'New institutions for transatlantic trade?' (*International Affairs*, January 1999); 'Is the Millennium Round worth reviving?' (*Zeitschrift für Wirtschaftspolitik*, March 2000); and 'Internationalization of Financial Services: a Trade-Policy Perspective' (in Stijn Claessens and Marion Jansen (eds), *The Internationalization of Financial Services*, Kluwer Law International for the WTO and the World Bank, London, 2000). The Centre for Policy Studies will shortly publish a piece by him, *Nice and After*, on the outcome of the Nice IGC.

Brian Hindley is British, but his AB (1961) and Ph.D. (1967) are both from the University of Chicago.

Martin Howe

Martin Howe is a practising Queen's Counsel specialising in European law and intellectual property law, who conducts cases before the English courts, the European Court of Justice, and other European tribunals. Previous publications include *Europe and the Constitution after Maastricht* (Nelson & Pollard, Oxford, 1993); *Monetary Policy after Maastricht: How much independence will Britain possess?* (Centre for Policy Studies, 1992); *Maastricht and 'Social Europe': An escape or an entrapment?* (Nelson & Pollard, 1993); and *Recommendations for the Intergovernmental Conference* (CPS, 1996).

Martin Howe was appointed QC in 1996. He was called to the Bar (Middle Temple) in 1978. He has received the Everard ver Heyden Foundation Prize (1978); the Middle Temple Harmsworth Exhibition (1976); the Astbury Law Scholarship (1979); and MA (Cantab) and BA (Cantab; 1977) degrees.

PREFACE

European issues are high on the IEA's research agenda. In recent years it has published eight papers on such issues, most recently Professor Roland Vaubel's analysis of centralising tendencies in the EU (Hobart Paper 127), Professor Otmar Issing's discussion of the relationship between monetary union and political union (Occasional Paper 98) and an issue of *Economic Affairs* (summer 1996) devoted to European Monetary Union.

As the debate on Britain's relationship with other European countries has intensified, it has become clear that the costs and benefits of membership of the EU are implicit in that debate. The Institute therefore decided to commission a study which would try to make the costs and benefits explicit, quantifying them to the extent possible. Dr Brian Hindley, of the London School of Economics, an economist who specialises in trade matters, and Martin Howe, a Queen's Counsel who has been much involved in European legal and constitutional issues, were asked to write a paper on the subject. Rodney Leach, a prominent businessman who has given much thought to Britain's relationship with Europe, was invited to contribute a Foreword commenting on the study.

The authors' focus is on the costs and benefits of different forms of relationship between Britain and the rest of the EU, extending to the option – sometimes termed 'unthinkable' or 'suicidal' – of withdrawal from the Union. But their objective is not to recommend withdrawal. It is, by examining that extreme option, to demonstrate the likely consequences of changing Britain's relationship with the EU.

As it happens, their conclusion is that withdrawal – even in the unlikely event of there being no free trading agreement with the rest of the EU – would have a relatively minor impact on the British economy. Large benefits would accrue as British consumers escaped from the Common Agricultural Policy but there would be some offsetting losses from the greater difficulty of exporting to the EU and possibly from reduced overseas investment in Britain. On balance, there might be a small net cost or a small net benefit on items which can be measured. In addition, there might be net advantages to Britain from effects which cannot be quantified – for example, reduced EU regulation and reversion to the supremacy of UK (rather than EU) law.

Dr Hindley and Mr Howe conclude that it would be foolish to make a decision on Britain's relationship with Europe based on economic costs and benefits alone. But if the EU is developing along lines a British government finds unacceptable, '. . . fear of adverse economic consequences should not deter a British government from seeking to change the relationship of the UK with the EU, or, in the last resort, from leaving the Union' (p. 99).

As in all IEA publications, this paper represents the views of the authors, not of the Institute (which has no corporate view), its managing trustees, Academic Advisory Council members or senior staff.

COLIN ROBINSON
Editorial Director, Institute of Economic Affairs
Professor of Economics, University of Surrey
October 1996

FOREWORD TO THE NEW EDITION

For years British policy towards Europe has been based on comforting assumptions. Politically, it was assumed that Europe either did not mean, or could ultimately be deflected from, its federal ambitions. Economically, it was assumed that the benefits of the single market were so vast and so self-evident as to need no defence and warrant no analysis; and that these benefits would be lost if Britain changed its relationship with the European Union.

This IEA Occasional Paper challenges these economic assumptions, starting from three simple premises. First, that trade with the EU represents a relatively small proportion of British economic activity, most of which would survive withdrawal from the EU, let alone a negotiated restructuring of our relationship. Second, that the CAP costs Britain more than the maximum tariffs that could be charged to British exports by Europe even in the worst case (and highly unlikely) scenario of a breakdown of trade preference. Third, that there are significant costs associated with the current skewing of trade towards the EU.

This revised edition is timely, given that Maastricht, Amsterdam and Nice have stripped away the illusion that the EU has neared the high-water mark of integration. While until recently it was easy for British opponents of federalism to believe that the EU constituted a weighty economic plus, offset by manageable political irritations, it is increasingly arguable that both sides of the scale have shifted. Europe now seems to be, if not firmly set, at least embarked on a political course which is at odds with the wishes of most British voters, while the authors make out a plausible case that the benefits of the single market are sufficiently counteracted by compensating costs as to leave the overall economic balance of advantage doubtful.

The authors have not succumbed to naïve Eurosceptic preconceptions. For example, they do full justice to the risk that foreign direct investment in Britain might be deterred by withdrawal from the EU. Indeed, in their determination to stand only on solid ground they have omitted mention of the costs and benefits of economic and monetary union and have touched only lightly on the question of regulation – two topics on which the preponderance of evidence lies in favour of British independence from the main drift of EU policy.

Having entered the EEC late, painfully, perhaps under false pretences, but certainly at a time when membership of a free trade area or an extensive customs union conferred real advantages, it appears to the conventional mind almost unthinkable to contemplate an altered relationship today, when the interlocking European institutions are so entrenched in our system. Yet in the past the IEA has thought the unthinkable to redoubtable effect. And certain features of the world economy have now either changed or emerged with such clarity as to make it valuable to challenge our most cherished convictions.

The last fifteen years have seen the revitalisation of the USA, fuelled by liberal trading instincts, labour flexibility and faith in free markets. To some extent Europe has stood aside from these trends and has been rewarded with declining innovation, declining growth and structural unemployment. Britain has been an exception, resulting in an economic performance which in relative if not in absolute terms has been the best in living memory. This fine performance has reinforced belief across the British political spectrum in market-driven policies, in deregulation and in curtailed social costs, and therefore has tended to align our ways of thinking rather more to the Atlanticist viewpoint than to that of continental Europe. At the same time, successive GATT rounds have sharply reduced the value of belonging to a customs union.

An important part of this Occasional Paper is its analysis of alternative arrangements in the event that Britain and the EU were ever mutually to determine that the existing relationship is not sustainable. This has long been a taboo subject, on the grounds that even to contemplate the alternatives would be to give undue credence to the notion that Britain is a reluctant European. But once the possibility is admitted that Britain's ambition for retaining a high degree of independence might ultimately prove irreconcilable with the Commission's – and arguably Germany's and other countries' – wish for the substantial diminution of the role of the nation state, it is only sensible to review how the political aspirations of each of Europe's electorates could be met without sacrificing the benefits of close trade ties. The authors canvas a number of possible amicable alternatives, all of which would represent a significant improvement over an intemperate withdrawal or a resentful expulsion. There are, after all, interesting rival models, for example Switzerland and Norway.

Europe is often thought to be too complex a subject for the ordinary voter and the systematic over-statement of the economic advantages deriving from membership of the EU has led to an exaggerated respect for the views of official business bodies. Of course, one does not want to downplay the immense complexities of European history, which have given Germany, France, Spain, Italy and Britain such different legacies of trading patterns, of financial structures and above all of attitudes towards the great issues of the day, from protectionism to social and defence policies. But businessmen have no special insight into these questions, nor indeed is any particular business insight called for in evaluating the broad outlines of the economic pluses and minuses of membership of the EU. The facts more or less speak for themselves. It is only natural to assume that so vast a question as Britain's relationship with the EU must involve balancing large advantages and large disadvantages – prosperity as against loss of national identity, perhaps, or, for those of a sceptical persuasion, the risks of membership as against the cost of isolation. So it comes as a shock to be told (as much by objective Europhiles as by the IEA authors) that the economic decision is so close as to be effectively immaterial. In strictly financial terms, it seems, membership of the Community's customs union is far less important than whether we have the judgement to conduct our own economic affairs sensibly and whether our business leaders have the energy to exploit our advantages of language, respect for the rule of law, labour flexibility and cost competitiveness.

The currently conventional view is that come what may we must maintain our present relationship with the EU, hoping that the momentum towards federal integration peters out. But if these hopes are unfulfilled, then we shall be confronted with a new situation. It would be folly to enter such a new situation equipped only with prejudice about the costs and benefits of membership of the EU. This is the central issue addressed by the present IEA paper, which should be studied very carefully by all those, of whatever persuasion, who are interested in the truth.

RODNEY LEACH
Jardine Matheson
June 2001

SUMMARY

- A majority of other member-states may insist on a 'federalist' agenda for the EU that a British government (of either party) would find unacceptable.
- If that occurred, the economic costs and benefits of EU membership would be crucial in determining Britain's response.
- Britain has the effective legal power to secede from the EU: Parliament could terminate the enforceability of Community Law in the British courts. Withdrawal would more likely be by agreement than by a 'messy unilateral break'.
- Outside the EU, Britain might become a free-standing member of the world trading system, relying on WTO trading rules. More likely there would be some form of free-trading relationship with the rest of the EU.
- Many costs and benefits of EU membership are intangible. For instance, Britain may suffer from excessive EU regulation and from the more effective enforcement of single-market and other rules in British courts than elsewhere.
- An assessment of those costs and benefits which can be quantified suggests the net effect of withdrawal on the British economy would be small – probably less than 1 per cent of GDP. If a special relationship with the rest of the EU were arranged, there might be a small benefit.

- The major quantifiable cost of EU membership is adherence to the Common Agricultural Policy (CAP). Escape from the CAP would represent a clear gain to Britain.
- There would be some loss because of the imposition of tariff barriers on UK exports to the EU but, allowing for switching of exports to non-EU countries and other adjustments, it would be small.
- Some loss of inward foreign direct investment (FDI) might also occur, though Britain's flexible labour markets (rather than EU membership) may be the principal reason for much FDI.
- There is no foundation for the idea that UK departure from the EU would have 'dire economic consequences'. 'If the EU ... develops along lines that the UK finds unacceptable on fundamental political grounds, fear of adverse economic consequences should not deter a British government from seeking to change the relationship of the UK with the EU or, in the last resort, from leaving the Union.'

TABLES

GLOSSARY OF ABBREVIATIONS

AC	Appeal cases
CAP	Common Agricultural Policy
CFP	Common Fisheries Policy
CMLR	Common Market Law Reports
ECJ	European Court of Justice
ECR	European Court Reports
ECSC	European Steel and Coal Community
EEA	European Economic Area
EFTA	European Free Trade Area
FDI	Foreign direct investment
FTA	Free trade area
GATS	General Agreement on Trade in Services
GATT	General Agreement on Tariffs and Trade
HS	Harmonised System
IGC	Intergovernmental Conference
ITC	International Trade Commission
NAFTA	North American Free Trade Area
NIESR	National Institute of Economic and Social Research
OECD	Organisation for Economic Cooperation and Development
OJ	Official Journal of the European Communities
USITC	United States International Trade Commission
WTO	World Trade Organization

ACKNOWLEDGEMENTS

Brian Hindley received valuable comments on earlier drafts of this paper from Professor David Henderson and Dr Ray Richardson. Tiffany Cochran provided excellent research assistance on the revised version. None of these is responsible for remaining errors, and no policy position should be imputed to any of them on the basis of this acknowledgement.

B . H .

INTRODUCTION TO THE SECOND EDITION: THE SMALL EFFECT OF EU MEMBERSHIP ON BRITISH ECONOMIC WELFARE

Better Off Out? makes no confident statement about whether Britain gains or loses from membership of the EU (European Union). This lack of a firm conclusion attracted criticism from some readers of the first edition. The *Independent* of 18 October 1996 reported that:

> Mr FitzGerald (chairman of Unilever) singled out a recent study by the Institute of Economic Affairs for vilification. The study by Brian Hindley and Martin Howe concluded that 'it is in practice hard to tell whether leaving the EU "cold turkey" would make Britain better or worse off'. Mr FitzGerald said: 'This remarkable conclusion defies all the experience of what has happened in the past quarter century. It is a classic piece of economists' dither – on the one hand this, on the other hand that.'

Mr FitzGerald should have read on. He somehow missed the conclusion that *Better Off Out?* did reach, which is that the effect on British economic welfare of EU membership is small, relative to GDP, whether it is a gain or a loss. Mr FitzGerald, who had proclaimed the 'horrific economic consequences' of withdrawal in the *Financial Times* (5 June 1996) – who had said, in other words, that the economic effect of membership is very large – should have been able to understand the significance of the conclusion that it is small.

Attempts to address the economic costs and benefits of EU membership in a serious and balanced way face the problem that many reactions to the question seem to be based on preconceived general views about the attractiveness of the EU rather than on any serious consideration of the evidence. Those strongly in favour of Britain's involvement in ever greater European integration tend to believe that Britain obtains large economic gains from EU membership, without asking whether the evidence supports that conclusion. Indeed, they are often unwilling to entertain even the *possibility* that the economic benefits of membership are small. Such disbelief, of course, is a general human characteristic – most people give more weight to evidence or anecdotes that seem to support their beliefs than to evidence that challenges them.

It is a peculiarity of debate about the EU, though, that those who are strongly and emotionally in favour of European integration seem able to sustain a belief in large economic benefits without any supporting evidence at all, and in the face of mounting contrary evidence. They are, as the psychiatrists say, in denial. The claim that the benefits are large plays an important role in pro-integration arguments. But when challenged about the basis of this claim, they all too often merely re-affirm their belief – their faith – that the economic gains *must* be large. They do not point to a mass of serious and respectable studies underpinning that conclusion. They cannot. There are none.

That is not for lack of effort. Since the first edition of *Better Off Out?*, two relevant studies have appeared, one by the National Institute of Economic and Social Research[1], and a second by the

---

1   NIESR, 2000, *Continent Cut Off? The Macroeconomic Effects of British Withdrawal from the EU*, London, National Institute of Economic and Social Research, February.

United States International Trade Commission[2], as part of a study of the economic consequences of British membership of NAFTA (North American Free Trade Area).

The NIESR study is especially interesting. According to the *Financial Times* (18 February 2000), it was funded by 'the pro-European Britain in Europe group' and was intended to 'mark the start of a campaign . . . to try to convince the public of the benefits of EU membership'.

In the event, the NIESR study concludes (p. 6) that British real gross national income twenty years after withdrawal would be 1.5 per cent lower than if we had retained our membership. A fall in income of that magnitude is a quite a long way from catastrophe.[3] Even the 1.5 per cent, however, derives from assumptions that are debatable.

In particular, the NIESR study assumes that inward investment brings with it substantial technical progress, so that a reduction in foreign direct investment (FDI) in the UK

2   USITC, 2000, *The impact on the US economy of including the United Kingdom in a free trade arrangement with the US, Canada, and Mexico*, Washington DC, publication 3339, August.

3   Britain in Europe seems to have been less than completely happy with the number. The *Financial Times* reported (22 February 2000) that: 'The launch of the "Out of Europe, Out of Work" campaign was overshadowed by an apology from Britain in Europe for the way a report by the National Institute of Economic and Social Research, about the consequences of withdrawal, had been represented in sections of the press last week. Several supporters of Britain in Europe accused Simon Buckby, the group's campaign director, of putting too much "spin" on the institute's report. One newspaper claimed on Friday that 8m jobs could be lost through withdrawal, prompting the institute to issue a summary of its report containing the calculation that 3.2m jobs were related to the sale of goods and services in the EU.' Given the title of the campaign, the campaign manager's frustration is easily understandable. In fact, although the NIESR report says that 3.2m jobs are related to trade with the rest of the EU, it also says that withdrawal would cause the loss of very few of them, if any.

manufacturing sector, for example, lowers the rate of technical progress and labour productivity in the entire manufacturing sector. The 1.5 per cent reduction in output then follows from the additional assumption that re-imposition of tariffs between Britain and the rest of the EU will have large effects on inward FDI, and, hence, on technical progress in the British economy. As the NIESR (p. 35) itself admits, 'The main factor explaining the lower level of output [claimed by the study] is the reduction in technical progress arising from lower inward investment.'

The large effect on inward investment assumed by NIESR contrasts sharply with the findings of the USITC study, which are based on the USITC's own model of the world economy. NIESR (p. 28) claims that withdrawal from the EU will eventually reduce the real value of the [US] investment stock by almost two-thirds . . .'. The USITC, on the other hand, says (pp. 4–22) that: 'These small effects . . . [on inward investment] . . . contrast with the views of various UK academic trade specialists, business leaders, and government officials . . . many of whom believe that dramatic reductions in FDI would follow the UK's leaving the EU.'

The United States accounts for roughly half of the stock of foreign-owned capital in the United Kingdom (and Japan, the source of much threat and bluster about the consequences for inward FDI of various British policies, for about 3 per cent). NIESR's claim that US investment in Britain would dramatically decline following withdrawal is therefore a major prop for its finding that British real income would decline. On this matter, however, the contrary view of the USITC, which has an obvious interest in getting right the facts about US overseas investment, but no obvious interest in supporting one side or the other in the British debate, cannot be lightly dismissed.

The fall in inward investment claimed by NIESR would not lead to the fall in British real income reported by NIESR, however, without NIESR's other key assumption, which is that inward investment boosts technological progress in the economy as a whole. That inward investors – or, at least, that some inward investors – bring with them new techniques and know-how is plausible. That, however, does not lead to the NIESR result – in and of itself, superior know-how will simply lead to higher profits for the foreign investor, which are not, as such, a source of welfare gain for the British economy. The NIESR result comes from the assumption that the new techniques filter through to other companies and persons in the economy, so that they acquire the techniques sooner than they otherwise would. This, NIESR claims, is how inward investment raises the rate of technological progress in general, and multiplies the effect on British income of a fall in inward investment.

The existence of such spillover effects is not implausible in *a priori* terms. Nevertheless, the only detailed and disaggregated study of the effects of inward investment in Britain fails to find them. Girma, Greenaway and Wakelin comment (p. 20) that 'When we tested for intra-industry spillovers, we found that on average there were no wage and productivity spillovers to domestic firms as a result of foreign presence, whether in levels or growth.'[4]

Both of the questionable NIESR assumptions regarding inward investment are necessary for it to arrive at the result that

---

4   Girma, Greenaway and Wakelin, 2001, 'Who benefits from foreign ownership in the UK?', *Scottish Journal of Political Economy*, May, Vol. 28 (2). The authors do find differences in wages. 'Even after we allow for productivity differences we still find that foreign firms pay on average 5 per cent more than domestic firms. In terms of nationality, we found American firms to have the largest differential and Japanese firms the smallest.'

withdrawal will reduce British real income by 1.5 per cent. Had it dropped either of them, NIESR would have concluded that the effects on British income of withdrawal from the EU are in the region of zero.

This result is in line with the results of the USITC study. To be more exact, the conclusion that the costs of withdrawal are small can be inferred from the USITC study – the study does not aim to make determinations of that cost, and no result on it is explicitly stated. The USITC compares the *status quo* with two alternative scenarios:

a) Britain remains part of the EU and joins NAFTA;[5] and
b) Britain leaves the EU and joins NAFTA.

It is the difference between these two situations that offers a basis for inferring the effects of withdrawal from the EU in the absence of NAFTA membership that the USITC would have found, had that question been put to it.

---

5   The conceptual experiment of the ITC, however, risks practical confusion. Britain cannot in the real world join NAFTA and remain a member of the EU. In this context, the relevant fact about the EU is that it is a customs union, while NAFTA is a free trade area. Members of a customs union adopt a common tariff; members of a free trade area do not. Hence, in principle, goods may enter a customs union at any port of entry and can then move freely within the customs union: in principle, no customs posts are needed at internal borders. Customs posts are needed, though, even in principle, at the internal borders of a free trade area: otherwise goods will enter the free trade area through the country with the lowest tariff, and the higher tariffs of other members will exist only on paper. Moreover, a free trade area requires 'rules of origin', which tell customs inspectors whether goods arriving at the US border with Mexico, for example, are of US or Canadian origin, and therefore entitled to duty-free admission; or of other origin, and therefore subject to duty. Clearly, free movement of goods within the EU is a principle that the EU will not easily surrender. If Britain left the EU, however, it could enter a free trade area with the EU *and* be a member of NAFTA.

The difference might be a quite fragile foundation for inference were the effects of Britain joining NAFTA large. A situation can be imagined, for example, in which a large part of British economic activity is re-focused to the US as a consequence of joining NAFTA, even though Britain remains a member of the EU. In that event, the differential effect of leaving the EU while a member of NAFTA might be small; but the effect of leaving the EU in the absence of NAFTA membership large.

As the USITC figures turn out, however, the effects on Britain of either (a) or (b) are small. It can legitimately be inferred, therefore, that the effects of leaving the EU in the absence of NAFTA membership are small.

'The effects of the contemplated FTA [on] each country's GDP are very small,' the ITC says about situation (a): 'the UK's GDP increases by less than one tenth of one per cent . . .' (p. xiv). And of (b): 'As in scenario 1, the changes in GDP are very small. UK GDP falls by 0.02 per cent' (p. xv).

As matters stand, therefore, the two direct studies of the economic costs to Britain of withdrawal from the EU, *Better Off Out?* and NIESR, 2000, both find that the costs are small, and the USITC study implies the same result. Euro-integrators need to produce respectable evidence for their claim that the economic costs of withdrawal are large. If they cannot produce evidence, they should stop making the claim.

That the costs of withdrawal from the EU are small does not say that Britain should withdraw. It strongly suggests, though, that debate about Britain and the EU should turn on politics, not on economics.

Some took the first edition of *Better Off Out?* to be arguing for withdrawal from the EU. But it did not. It said that, as a matter of economics, withdrawal was neither infeasible nor unthinkable. Therefore it ought not to be dismissed as a practical option for the nation, if membership imposes conditions that the country finds onerous. The first edition did not argue for withdrawal, and neither does this edition.

Note on the revised edition

In this edition, the 1994 figures from the original are updated to 1998, the latest year for which all figures are available. We have followed the methods of calculation employed in the original edition. Alterations in the text are on the level of copy-editing, except where it seems important to incorporate new information or where information or statistics that appeared in the original version are no longer available.[6]

---

6   So that, for example, Table 5 in the original, which gives a breakdown of foreign credits and debits for various service industries, does not appear in this edition – the necessary statistics do not appear to be available.

1 INTRODUCTION: REASONS TO ASSESS THE COSTS AND BENEFITS OF BRITAIN'S EU MEMBERSHIP

The debate

In Britain, both main political parties at least nominally adhere to the position that the United Kingdom should remain a sovereign, independent nation state. The 1992–7 Parliament was a period which saw widely publicised differences of opinion over the ratification of the Maastricht Treaty and over Britain's subsequent relationship with the EU. Media attention was mainly focused on the differences of view within the Conservative party and government, but differences of policy also existed within the Labour Party, which had twice reversed its position over whether we should belong to the EEC at all since we joined in 1973.

Divisions within the political parties, of course, reflect divisions within British society at large. Even constituencies whose members might have been expected to hold positions roughly consistent with one another, such as senior businessmen, cover a broad spectrum.

Sir Stanley Kalms, chairman of Dixons, for example, has commented that:

> This draft directive [on consumer guarantees] is
> symptomatic of the tide of regulations coming out of
> Brussels that threaten to limit our economic success. It is
> preposterous that nowhere in the European Commission's

proposals is consideration given to their cost. No fair-minded person would object to reasonable regulation . . . but in recent years the balance has shifted. What we are seeing is the concept of harmonisation developing into a major assault on the long-established principles of economic supply and demand. It will be a sterile debate when, in five or six years' time, we consider the consequences of joining a single currency if British industry has already suffered death by a thousand cuts.[1]

On the other hand, Mr Niall FitzGerald, chairman-designate (now chairman) of Unilever, has expressed concern about:

. . . those siren voices who wish to lure us on to the rocks of withdrawal. It angers me when politicians in particular indulge themselves in such talk without taking any responsibility for the horrific economic consequences of such a step . . . it is irresponsible and self-indulgent to claim that there is a serious case for withdrawal and then to choose to ignore the reality of the economic consequences.[2]

Why the economic costs and benefits should be assessed

The debate in Britain about the European Union has both political and economic dimensions. The Conservative Party is now firmly committed to a position of robust defence of Britain's national sovereignty against further extensions of EU powers, and the promotion of an open, flexible European structure. The Labour Party is more willing to accept further extensions to EU powers, particularly in the social field, arguing that such extensions are still

---

1   *The Times*, 17 August 1996.
2   *Financial Times*, 5 June 1996.

compatible with maintaining national sovereignty. But despite the difference in emphasis between them, both major parties may sooner or later have to face up to the question of how they can reconcile the continued status of Britain as a nation state with the ongoing process of EU integration. However, it seems clear that the governments of most, if not all, other member-states favour construction of an overtly federal European Union, ultimately becoming a 'United States of Europe'.

Both parties may therefore have cause before too long to think more deeply than they have about the whole question of Britain's relationship with the EU.The Nice summit meeting in December 2000 was significant not only for the further steps of European integration which were agreed, but also for what was agreed regarding further steps. A declaration[3] of enormous importance was agreed. This states that by 2004 there will be yet another Intergovernmental Conference (IGC) to draw up yet another treaty. That IGC will undertake a 'deeper and wider debate about the future development of the European Union'. The first question the 2004 IGC will address is how to 'establish and monitor a more precise delimitation of competencies' between the European Union and the member states. It will also consider the role of national Parliaments in the European architecture.

For a powerful strand of thinking amongst continental politicians, the 2004 IGC will provide the opportunity for the formal creation of a constitution for the European Union. Politicians of such persuasion make no secret of their wish to see the European Union increasingly assume the powers and trappings of a State. Joschka Fischer's Humboldt University speech in May 2000 was

---

3   Declaration on the Future of the Union annexed to the Final Act of the Conference, 26 February 2001.

one of the most explicit and widely publicised statements to this effect.

There is a real prospect that the majority of other member-states may persist in advancing a 'federalist' agenda that a British government of either party will want to reject. If that happens, the economic costs and benefits of membership of the European Union may become a crucial element in framing Britain's response. If membership of the European Union is indeed essential to Britain's economic well-being, then going along with developments of the European Union even though they are thought politically undesirable might seem the lesser of two evils. On the other hand, if the net economic benefits of Britain's membership are modest, neutral or even negative, then Britain can afford to be far more robust. It might then, for example, feel far less inhibited in vetoing political developments of the European Union which it does not like, or at least in pressing for exclusion from them and possibly for a special status outside an 'inner core' of more federally committed member-states.

Thus, in our view, an assessment of the economic costs and benefits of Britain's membership of the European Union is an essential precondition to forming national policy on the fundamental question of: 'What kind of European Union do we wish to belong to?'

European monetary union

The costs and benefits of European monetary union would occupy a paper – indeed, volumes of papers – in themselves.[4] At present,

---

4 A symposium on the subject of monetary union is in *Economic Affairs*, Vol. 16, No. 3, summer 1996. See also Pedro Schwartz, *Back from the Brink*, Occasional

the United Kingdom retains the right to decide whether or not to participate in the single currency, and the pros and cons of that separate decision require separate analysis.

However, increasing political pressure on the UK is likely to arise if it remains opted out from the single currency, on the grounds that it is unfairly taking advantage of the benefits of access to the single market but is not subject to constraints against competitive devaluations. The Treaty basis of the single market was laid down well before the European Monetary Union project, and the UK's right to participate in the single market is not linked to or dependent upon participation in the European single currency.

Nevertheless, legal norms in the EU are bendable rather than fixed, particularly in the direction which favours the prevailing political climate in favour of greater European integration. Thus, if the UK stays outside the single currency it may face increasing attempts to restrict its freedom of action in its exchange rate management,[5] or to subject it to disadvantages in the single market as compared with the 'in' countries. That is a further reason for attempting to assess the costs and benefits of Britain's EU membership.

Assessing costs and benefits

In order to assess these costs and benefits, it is necessary to compare the current position with the position Britain would be in if it

---

Paper 101, IEA, 1997; Michael Portillo, *Democratic Values and the Currency*, Occasional Paper 103, IEA, 1998; and Michael Bordo and Lars Jonung, *Lessons for EMU from the History of Monetary Unions*, Readings 50, IEA, 2000.

5   See Martin Howe, 'Monetary Policy after Maastricht: How much independence will Britain possess?', London, Centre for Policy Studies, November 1992.

were not a member of the EU and were instead a free-standing member of the multilateral world trading system. It is also necessary to address the (legal and constitutional) question of whether Britain would be able to withdraw from the European Union were it to wish to do so. That is not the same as advocating withdrawal as a policy. But we emphatically disagree with the claim that serious discussion of the effects and consequences of withdrawal should be a taboo subject. If the economic consequences of that step are 'horrific' and there is no 'serious case', then serious analysis of the issue can only serve to provide objective reinforcement for that viewpoint.

Political and economic issues

Britain's membership of the European Union and its position in its future development involve both political and economic costs and benefits. Both kinds of cost and benefit will play a part in any decisions that a British government, and Parliament, may take. Political issues are just as important as, and arguably far more important than, economic issues. However, political costs and benefits are in general not measurable.

For example, it is argued that, through being a member of a larger and more powerful bloc, Britain enhances its power in world affairs. On the other hand, by being a member of that bloc, Britain loses significant rights and powers over the way in which it governs itself domestically and over the way in which it conducts its external affairs. There is no way in which such benefits and costs can be quantified and weighed against each other.

Similarly, it is argued that the EEC, and now the EU, have contributed to maintaining peace in Europe. On the other hand, it is argued by some that the structures of the EU, by seeking to impose central rules on divergent nations, will ultimately be a cause of conflict rather than a solution to conflict. Such political questions cannot be weighed in quantitative terms, even though they are clearly important to any decisions which Britain takes about its future in Europe.

The discussion in this Occasional Paper is therefore confined to *economic* costs and benefits. Some of these, such as net budget contributions and the cost of tariffs saved are, at least in principle, quantifiable. Other costs and benefits are real and substantial but difficult to quantify. In this category are the intangible (but real) benefits of having a harmonised single market, as against the costs of the regulation which goes hand in hand with the harmonised market under the European system. These categories of cost and benefit do not admit of ready quantification, but the Paper attempts to assess them in qualitative terms.

A cultural difference in approach to markets

An important matter underlying the economic costs and benefits of EU membership is an apparent cultural difference in attitudes to free markets between the 'Anglo-Saxon' and the 'continental' approaches. The latter exhibits a propensity to favour regulation over free markets. A more federal structure would allow this propensity freer rein, creating what many British voters, even enthusiasts for the single market, might regard as a noxious mixture. As the article by Sir Stanley Kalms cited on p. 31 suggests, however, the problem is real even within the present European structure. Two examples suffice to illustrate the underlying issue.

The first is a report in *The Times* (8 December 1993) in the run-up to the 1994 elections for the European Parliament, under the headline: 'Tories embarrassed by European allies'. The allies are the European People's Party (EPP), with which the Conservatives are associated in the European Parliament. The problem lay in the draft EPP manifesto for the elections. One sentence conveys the flavour of the manifesto and explains the embarrassment. It says that 'governments must ensure that the functioning of the market remains subordinate to the general welfare and social justice'.

That free markets are better for the general welfare than political processes is, of course, the central proposition of classical liberal thought. British Conservatives do not always apply it in full, but few of them would deny its force or fail to pay it at least lip service. That their continental counterparts refuse even lip service reveals an intellectual gulf. Reflected in policy, it could become a political chasm.

The second example underlines the first. It comes from a *Financial Times* report (31 December 1993) of an interview with M Edouard Balladur, then Prime Minister of France. 'What is the market?', M Balladur is reported as saying. 'It is the law of the jungle, the law of nature. And what is civilisation? It is the struggle against nature.'

The European People's Party and M Balladur are 'right-of-centre' in continental terms. If they reject the market, that strongly suggests that there is and will for the foreseeable future be an inherent EU bias towards non-market solutions – towards statist regulation.[6] The problem of the costs imposed by European-style

---

6   There are classical economic liberals on the continent, of course. Roland Vaubel, Professor of Economics at the University of Mannheim, for example, presents a superb piece of liberal reasoning and exposition in *The Centralisation of Western Europe*, Hobart Paper 127, London, Institute of Economic Affairs, 1995.

regulation therefore seems likely to grow in importance in the future.

Costing membership and the meaning of 'withdrawal'

No reliable assessment of the costs of withdrawal from the European Union is publicly available, and none may exist. Indeed, the preliminary spadework that might make accurate estimation possible has not been done. To estimate the costs and benefits of a policy, what would happen if the policy is pursued must be compared with what would happen if it is not. In the case in hand, Britain's economic circumstances as a member of the EU must be compared with its economic circumstances if it withdraws from the EU. 'Withdrawal from the EU', however, has no single simple meaning.

Withdrawal might mean, for example, that membership was not replaced by any special arrangement between independent Britain and the EU. In that event, trade and other economic relations between the two would be controlled by multilateral agreements such as those under the World Trade Organization (WTO) – that is, by arrangements similar to those that now govern economic relations between the EU and the USA, or between the EU and Australia.

That, however, should tentatively be regarded as the worst case. It is sometimes assumed that British departure from the EU would lead the remaining members to act punitively towards Britain. That seems unlikely – but even if it were true, the WTO provides a bottom line for actions the EU could legally take with respect to an independent Britain. Other arrangements seem likely to be available. The EU has a variety of preferential trading arrangements with neighbouring non-members. It would be surprising if such arrangements were not available for Britain, for reasons to do with the self-interest of the remaining EU members which are discussed in Chapter 3 later.

Organisation of the Paper

Chapter 2 discusses the structure and framework of the European single market, and compares its main features with the world multilateral trading system. Chapter 3 then goes on to consider some possible legal frameworks for relations between the EU and a departed Britain, and their advantages and disadvantages.

An attempt at assessing the economic costs and benefits of withdrawal is presented in Chapter 4. Following that, conclusions and comments are presented in Chapter 5.

Inevitably, analysis of the kind presented here has a number of technical aspects. But technicality distracts from the thrust of the main argument, so such matters are covered – to the extent possible – in two appendices, one on economic issues and one on legal matters.

2 THE EC SINGLE MARKET AND THE WORLD TRADING SYSTEM

The 'internal' market in the context of the European Union

The greatest perceived benefit of Britain's membership of the EU is access to the European 'internal' market for British exporters of goods and services. Against this perceived benefit, however, must be set what are generally seen as disadvantages to Britain flowing from other aspects of membership of the EU, such as the cost burdens imposed by European social legislation and the costs to consumers and taxpayers of the Common Agricultural Policy (CAP).

However, the purpose of this chapter is to try to assess the benefit to Britain that arises from the single market itself. This will involve consideration both of the substantive rules which regulate that market, and of the enforcement mechanisms which exist to ensure that the degree of market access laid down on paper is achieved in practice. With regard to the latter point, despite criticisms of the European Court of Justice (ECJ) made in other contexts, its expansive techniques of interpretation are widely regarded as beneficial to Britain in the single market context, because these techniques are seen as resulting in 'strong' enforcement of Community free-trading rules.[1] In the course of

---

1   Indeed, this belief led the former Conservative British Government to propose

considering the benefits and costs of the single market, that proposition will be subject to critical examination.

The objective of creating the single market is laid down by Article 14 of the Treaty of Rome.[2] The single market is defined as 'an area without frontiers in which the free movement of goods, persons, services and capital is ensured in accordance with the provisions of this Treaty'. The single market, whose construction was laid down as a Community objective by the Single European Act of 1986, is the successor to the 'common market' of the original Rome Treaty, upon which it builds.

In practical terms, as regards the free movement of goods, the single market has involved the abolition of customs formalities between member-states since the beginning of 1993. This carries the single market a stage beyond the common market or customs union, where customs formalities existed at the borders between member-states but tariffs levied were zero. The basic elements of the single market are thus:

- No customs formalities relating to the movement of goods between member-states and therefore, by definition, no tariffs
- No quotas on trade between member-states
- A general prohibition, under Articles 28 to 30[3] of the Rome Treaty and the case law of the ECJ developed under those

---

the inclusion in the Maastricht Treaty of a provision strengthening the powers of the European Court of Justice by empowering it to fine member-states which disregarded its judgments: Rome Treaty, Article 171(2) as amended by Maastricht, since renumbered as Article 228(2).

2   This was inserted into the Treaty of Rome as Article 8a by the Single European Act and renumbered by Maastricht as Article 7a.

3   Formerly numbered articles 30 to 36.

Articles, against measures having 'equivalent effect' to quantitative restrictions
- A wide range of specific harmonisation measures which seek to impose uniform standards on goods placed on the European single market
- A series of 'harmonisation measures' in services
- In services, general restrictions against unjustified discrimination against nationals of other member-states, and general rights of establishment and movement in order to provide services
- Controls over unfair state subsidies and discriminatory public procurement practices

Construction of the European single market is based on several principles or 'rights', most of which date from the original common market, but in addition it has entailed heavy use of 'harmonisation'. The theory is that, in order to permit the free movement of goods across barrier-free borders, it is necessary for all member-states to have essentially the same minimum standards of product safety, technical standards, and so on. Otherwise, goods (or services) which would be unacceptable to some member-states are in free circulation in the single market.

'Harmonisation' as practised in Europe has benefits, but it also has costs. The benefit is that a manufacturer in any European country can manufacture goods to the common European standard in the expectation (in theory at least) that he will not then have to meet different or additional standards or requirements in order to export into any member-state. The cost is that the standards adopted may be unnecessarily cumbersome and expensive for the home market and for exports outside the

EC,[4] or may simply be inappropriate for the specific requirements of the home market or the country's industry.

The political problem with harmonisation is that many member-states are unwilling to accept less stringent standards than those which already apply in their own national markets. This leads to 'gold plating' of harmonisation directives under which the whole Community ends up adopting highly detailed and often excessive standards for its goods. This approach to constructing a single market has led to many thousands of pages of detailed harmonisation legislation. The direct cost is compliance with unnecessary standards in the domestic market and other EC markets, and possible loss of competitiveness in world markets. In essence, the economic problem posed by this technique of detailed, regulatory construction of a single market is that, in order to benefit that part of the national economy which consists of export of goods and services to the EC (about 14 per cent[5]), potentially 100 per cent of the economy is subjected to the regulatory régime. The cost of regulation across the economy as a whole therefore needs to be balanced against the benefit of single-market access for the EC exporting sector.

To take one small example amongst hundreds of possible instances, a 1994 Directive relating to the packaging of goods[6] seeks to curb the unnecessary use of packaging and generation of pack-

---

4   The distinction between the European Union (EU) and the European Community (EC) is explained on pages 46–7.

5   See Chapter 5 (p. 93).

6   Directive 94/62 of 20 December 1994, 'On Packaging and Packaging Waste' (*OJ* 1994, L365/10). This Directive was made under Article 95 (formerly 100a) of the Treaty of Rome (harmonisation of national measures affecting the single market).

aging waste on environmental grounds. It is complex[7] and has needed to be transposed into voluminous implementing regulations in the UK and in other member-states. It is a 'framework Directive' which provides for the making at the European level of further detailed subordinate legislation.[8] It will impose substantial burdens on producers, as well as administrative costs; however, if producers comply with its provisions, then (in theory at least) their products should be free to circulate into other member-states without being hindered by other locally differing packaging regulations.

Is the UK better off within this régime or outside it? For producers who do not export to other EC member-states, these regulations represent an unnecessary cost. For producers who do export there, it avoids the potential necessity to produce goods with two different standards of packaging, one for the home market and one for the EC. Whilst in theory it might be possible to attempt some form of quantification of these costs and benefits, the task would be difficult, and performing similar exercises Directive by Directive and sector by sector is not feasible.

It is not possible to assess quantitatively whether or not the benefits outweigh the costs of harmonisation, nor is it intuitively

---

7   It requires that all packaging shall fulfil 'essential requirements' (Article 9 and Annex 11) of minimum quantity used consistent with safety and hygiene of the consumer, that it shall be recyclable, and not contain hazardous or noxious substances. It requires member-states to attain targets for the recycling of packaging waste (Article 6: 50 per cent after five years). It requires the establishment of return, collection and recovery systems (Article 7) and imposes requirements for the compulsory marking and identification of packaging (Article 8).

8   The Directive provides for the Commission to lay down detailed standards relating to the packaging of particular products (Article 10) and to determine technical measures (Article 20). The Commission legislates under a procedure which also involves a Committee of representatives of the member-states (Article 21).

obvious that the costs or the benefits will predominate. They are likely to affect individual businesses in different ways depending on their own circumstances, and this may indeed be one reason for the sharp divergence of views among businessmen quoted in Chapter 1. In the absence of a method of measuring such costs and benefits, or strong consensus one way or the other amongst the businesses affected, it cannot be demonstrated that 'harmonisation' can, all in all, be regarded either as a net cost or a net benefit of belonging to the EC single market.

As regards services, a similar approach of detailed harmonisation is being progressively adopted to that applied to goods, but the process is far less complete. Thus, sector-by-sector harmonising directives have been issued. Again, the theory is that, once providers of services satisfy a common European standard (for example, of solvency in the context of financial services), they should then be free to offer services across the Community. There has been far less success in opening up the single market to British exporters of services than was hoped at the time of the Single European Act, and the 'gold plating' of harmonisation directives is just as much a problem as in manufactured goods.[9]

The single market in the context of the European Union

Although the single market is important, it is only one of the activities of the European Union. It is debatable whether or not it is now the central activity: clearly it is not as central as was the common market in the scheme of the original Treaty of Rome.

---

9   A good example is the Capital Adequacy Directive in the financial services sector, which has imposed standards on the British financial services sector which are widely perceived as cumbersome and unnecessary.

Thus, the activities of the European Union as such are not particularly relevant to trade or to the single market. Under the so-called 'three-pillared' structure of the Maastricht Treaty, the European Union engages in two fields of activity outside the ambit of the European Communities – the Common Foreign and Security Policy under Title V of Maastricht, and Justice and Home Affairs Co-operation under Title VI. Participation in these joint activities carries with it potential advantages and disadvantages of a political nature, which are not susceptible of being weighed in an economic analysis.

The first or original 'pillar' of the European Union is formed by the European Communities. These consist (confusingly) of the European Community (formerly European Economic Community or EEC, but with the word 'Economic' formally dropped by the Maastricht Treaty), the original European Coal and Steel Community (ECSC), and Euratom. The legal structures of the three European Communities are now essentially integrated with each other, and therefore ECSC and Euratom do not call for further separate consideration.

Apart from the single market itself, the activities of the EC include extensive European social legislation, environmental policies, the Common Agricultural Policy and, of course, the creation of a single European currency. The whole is intended to form part of 'the process of creating an ever closer union amongst the peoples of Europe'.[10] Therefore, the single-market measures and their methods and mechanisms of enforcement cannot be viewed in isolation as if they were contained in a free-standing international agreement whose purpose is the formation of a European single

---

10   Maastricht Treaty (Treaty on European Union), Article 1.

market. Instead they must be viewed, and their benefits and costs assessed, as forming part of a structure with a wider context and with an overarching political, rather than economic, purpose.

The Community legal order

The European Community possesses its own 'legal order'. In this rests the fundamental distinction between the EC and other international trade arrangements such as GATT, which operate at the level of relations between states. The legal order is embodied in Community law, a body of legal rules contained in, or made under, the Community Treaties.

Community law penetrates into the internal legal systems of the member-states and creates rights and obligations which are directly enforceable by and against businesses and private citizens. It is interpreted and ultimately enforced by the Communities' own institutions, paramount amongst which is the European Court of Justice (ECJ) in Luxembourg.

That Court itself clearly defined the nature of Community law in the early and seminal leading case of *Van Gend en Loos* in 1963.[11]

> This Treaty [of Rome] is more than an agreement which merely creates mutual obligations between the contracting states. This view is confirmed by the preamble to the Treaty which refers not only to governments but to peoples . . . the Community constitutes a new legal order in international law for whose benefit the states have limited their sovereign rights, albeit within limited fields, and the subjects of which comprise not only the Member-states but also their nationals.

---

11   Case 26/62 [1963] ECR 1; [1963] CMLR 105.

Community rules are enforced in three different ways. First, the European Commission has the task of policing compliance with the Treaties (and subordinate instruments such as directives made under them). If the Commission considers that a member-state is in breach of its obligations, it may initiate proceedings against the state before the ECJ under Article 226 of the Treaty. If a state fails to comply with a judgment of the Court requiring it to remedy a breach, it may ultimately be fined.[12] It is arguable that this method of enforcement is analogous to the methods of enforcement of international agreements, although the difference is in the presence of a 'policeman' in the form of the Commission. By contrast, for example, the World Trade Organization (WTO) cannot initiate complaints against member-states: only other member-states can do that.

Second, in certain fields Community rules are enforced by the direct supervisory action of a supranational institution, the Commission, acting within member-states against specific businesses and individuals. This is important in competition law and in relation to state subsidies.

The third and probably in many ways the most important method of enforcement of Community rules is through the national legal systems of the member-states. Rather surprisingly, this aspect of Community law is not explicitly spelt out in the Treaty of Rome or other Community treaties, but has been developed through interpretation of the Treaty by the ECJ in the Van Gend en Loos case quoted above, and in a whole series of further decisions. It is now a well-established feature of the EC.

---

12 Article 228(2), formerly 171(2) as amended (at British insistence) by the Maastricht Treaty.

The ECJ has made clear that national courts must directly apply Community law in preference to their own national laws in the event of a conflict, even if this involves overriding the fundamental or constitutional law of their own country. It follows that both governmental and national legislative acts, including (in the UK) even Acts of Parliament, must be struck down if they conflict with Community law. As Mr Justice Hoffmann said in the *Stoke-on-Trent* case[13] in 1990:

> The Treaty of Rome is the supreme law of this country,
> taking precedence over Acts of Parliament. Our entry into
> the Community meant that (subject to our undoubted but
> probably theoretical right to withdraw from the Community
> altogether) Parliament surrendered its sovereign right to
> legislate contrary to the Treaty on the matters of social and
> economic policy which it regulated.

The legal systems of the other member-states of the EC have in general accepted the principle of the supremacy of Community law as enunciated by the ECJ, although most ultimately reserve the right to make their own basic constitutional principles prevail in their own courts if there is a conflict between EC law and those principles, as distinct from ordinary national laws. In terms of day-to-day application of single-market rules, the position (at least theoretically) in all member-states is that national courts will accept the overriding effect of Community law. This potentially gives to individuals and businesses a direct means of enforcement of single-market rules.

Interpretation of both the content and the scope of Community law is a matter ultimately not for the national courts or authorities, but for the ECJ. The ECJ performs this function on a

---

13   [1990] 3 CMLR 31 at 34.

'reference' from a national court under Article 234 of the Rome Treaty. This is effectively an appeal from the national court to the ECJ in all but name.

In this aspect of Community law, its direct effect, the European Communities display some of the features of a federal state. Sovereignty is exercised within certain fields by the central authorities to the exclusion of the local or provincial authorities. Federal laws apply directly within all units of the federal state and override any local laws with which they conflict. The content and scope of federal laws, and the consequent restriction on the scope of autonomy of the lower units, is determined not by the lower units but by the organs of the federal authorities, most importantly by what is effectively the supreme constitutional court, the ECJ.

What implications does this have for the trading and other economic interests of the UK? A strong enforcement mechanism for Community rules might appear to be in the interests of the UK since it may limit the ability of other member-states to put up unfair and unlawful barriers to trade. However, this *prima facie* view must be subjected to critical examination, since the effectiveness of Community law in promoting British trading and economic interests within the EC is dependent both on the content of that law, and on how it is interpreted and enforced at European level, and at ground level within individual member-states.

Interestingly, the Court itself explained its approach to its interpretative role in the clearest possible terms when it compared the proposed European Economic Area Agreement[14] with the Treaty of Rome:

---

14 *Re Draft Treaty on a European Economic Area*: Opinion 1/91 [1992] 1 CMLR 245. The structure of the EEA agreement is considered in more detail in Chapter 3 (below, pp. 64–6).

An international treaty is to be interpreted not only on the basis of its wording, but in the light of its objectives . . . The Rome Treaty aims to achieve economic integration leading to the establishment of an internal market and economic and monetary union. Article 1 of the Single European Act makes it clear that the objective of all the Community treaties is to contribute together to making concrete progress towards European unity. It follows from the foregoing that the provisions of the Rome Treaty on free movement and competition, far from being an end in themselves, are only means for attaining those objectives.

The EEA is to be established on the basis of an international treaty which, essentially, merely creates rights and obligations as between its members and provides for no transfer of sovereign rights to the inter-governmental institutions which it sets up. In contrast, the Rome Treaty, albeit concluded in the form of an international agreement, none the less constitutes the constitutional charter of a Community based on the rule of law. As the Court of Justice has consistently held, the Community treaties established a new legal order for the benefit of which the States have limited their sovereign rights, in ever wider fields,[15] and the subjects of which comprise not only the member states but also their nationals. The essential characteristics of the Community legal order which has been thus established are in particular its primacy over the law of the member-states and the direct effect of a whole series of provisions which are applicable to their nationals and to the member-states themselves.

Because of the differences in the fundamental nature of the two

---

15   In the *Van Gend* case in 1963, the ECJ referred to the member-states having limited their sovereign rights in *limited fields*, but by the time of the EEA Treaty case in 1991 this had changed to '*ever wider fields*'.

treaties, the Court concluded that the corresponding parts of the EEA treaty and the Treaty of Rome on free movement and competition, even though identically worded, would be interpreted differently. By reaching this conclusion, the Court was in effect making a comment on its own technique of interpreting the Community treaties, which is to interpret them in such a way as best 'to make concrete progress towards European union', and on the presupposition that Community law will expand into 'ever wider fields'.

Rules of Community law pertaining to the free market are increasingly likely to be interpreted not with the objective of creating a single market free of barriers uppermost in mind, but with other factors predominating. During the early years, when establishment of the common market was the central objective of the EEC, the jurisprudence of the ECJ went strongly in the direction of freedom of trade. However, there has been an observable shift in more recent years away from free trade and towards other factors. For example, the ECJ has altered its earlier very broad interpretations in order to adopt a more restrictive scope for the application of Article 28, which prohibits quantitative restrictions on imports or measures having equivalent effect.[16] In the intellectual property field, the Court has dramatically reversed an earlier decision in order to give greater weight to the protection of intellectual prop-

---

16 *Keck and Daniel Mithouard*, Case C-267,8/91 [1995] 1 CMLR 101, restricted the applications of Articles 30 to 36 (since renumbered Articles 28 to 30) of the Treaty of Rome so that they no longer cover many trading rules which had previously been thought to be covered under the ECJ's earlier jurisprudence in *Procureur du Roi v. Dassonville*, Case 8/74 [1974] 2 CMLR 436, and the Cassis de Dijon case (*Rewe-Zentral v. Bundes-monopolverwaltung fur Branntwein*), Case 120/78 [1979] 3 CMLR 494.

erty rights and less to the principle of free movement of goods.[17]

And although the early jurisprudence of the ECJ achieved great progress in liberalising trade internally within the EC market, recent years have seen a strong tendency for the EC institutions to impose *restrictions* on freedom of trade between the UK (and other member-states) and the outside world. An important example is the ECJ's decision in the *Silhouette* case,[18] which interpreted the Trade Marks Directive[19] as requiring member-states to prohibit so-called 'parallel imports' of genuine trade-marked goods from non-member-states when the proprietor of the mark has not consented to the marketing of his goods within the Community. This enables trade mark proprietors to prevent the importation of their own genuine goods into the EC from other countries where they have placed them on the market (e.g. the USA), so enabling them to charge consumers within the EC a higher price than in other markets. A remarkable feature about the Silhouette judgment is that it arose from a *casus omissus* – a point which the Directive did not explicitly deal with – and the ECJ instinctively reached a conclusion which suggests that its basic mental furniture – its underlying preconceptions – tend towards Fortress Europe rather than global free trade.

A further important example of this tendency was exhibited by the ECJ in the field of regulations and technical standards.[20] This case concerned the British Ministry of Agriculture's practice of

17 *CNL-Sucal v. Hag GF AG*, Case C-10/89 [1990] ECR I-3711, reversing *Van Zuylen Freres v. Hag*, Case 192/73 [1974] 2 CMLR 127.

18 Case C-355/96 *Silhouette International Schmied GmbH v. Hartlauer Handelsgesellschaft mbH* [1998] 2 CMLR 953.

19 First Council Directive 89/104/EEC to approximate the laws of the member-states relating to trade marks.

20 Case C-100/96 *R v. MAFF ex p British Agrochemicals Association* [1999] ECR I-1499.

granting agrochemical licences to 'parallel imports' of products from third countries which were identical to, and from the same manufacturer as, agrochemicals licensed here. There is no objective reason for preventing imports of such identical products on safety or environmental grounds, although of course the manufacturers have a strong interest in maintaining higher prices within the EC market as compared with markets in other countries. Although the ministry would have been obliged by EC law to grant licences to similar parallel imports if they had been from other EC member-states, the ECJ ruled that these principles were not applicable in the case of imports from third countries and that the grant of the licences for third-country imports was actually *prohibited* by Community law. It said,[21] 'Nor does there exist, at international level, any general principle of the free movement of goods comparable to that prevailing within the Community.' It is impossible to see how this arbitrary discrimination against identical products imported from outside the EC can be compatible with the obligations of the UK and the EC itself under the WTO Agreement and the Agreement on Technical Barriers to Trade.[22] Therefore we see an example of the UK actually being forced by the EC to act in an anti-free trade manner and in breach of its obligations under the WTO Agreements, contrary to the UK's own strong interest in promoting free and non-discriminatory global trade.

Thus, the special or unique character of the method of enforcement of EC single-market rules is double-edged. The Community legal order, and the supremacy of Community law and its direct enforceability in national courts, mean that those rules may

---

21 In paragraph 44 of the judgment (at p. 1536).

22 For a brief description of this Agreement, see Appendix B.

be enforced more effectively than comparable rules which are merely part of an international treaty structure. However, the rules themselves may be interpreted differently, and with less of an eye to the importance of securing free trade as an objective, from the way they would be interpreted if they were not embodied in the broader political structure of the Treaties which establish the European Communities and the European Union.

A further aspect to consider, when considering the enforce-ability of single-market rules as relevant to the economic interests of the UK, is the extent to which disparities between national legal systems may differentially affect the extent to which single-market rules are enforced within different countries. Since Community law creates its direct effect by grafting itself on to the national legal systems of the member-states, its effectiveness depends on the ef-fectiveness or otherwise of the national legal system and on the willingness of the courts in each country to embrace and enthusi-astically enforce norms of Community law as distinct from merely paying lip service to it.

The legal system of the UK is highly effective, measured in terms of securing general obedience to legal rules by both the pri-vate sector and agencies of the government. It has also lent itself to the full application of norms of Community law. Indeed, a number of the senior judiciary are overt in their positive enthusiasm for Community law and its principles. This means that enforcement of single-market and other Community rules within the UK by pri-vate action can be extremely effective.

A good illustration is the Spanish fishing episode. Council Reg-ulation 170/83, implementing the Common Fisheries Policy (CFP), uses the criterion of the flag of registration of the fishing vessel to decide which national quota its catch shall count against. From about 1980 onwards, increasing numbers of Spanish vessels were re-registered as British vessels under the Merchant Shipping Act 1894, which was very permissive as to the effective nationality of the owners of vessels which could be registered as British. This practice was known as 'quota hopping', since it permitted the re-registered Spanish vessels to fish against the UK fisheries quota to the detriment of the British fishing industry. The Ministry of Agriculture and Fisheries became concerned at this practice, and made an initial attempt to curb it through fisheries licence conditions, but this proved ineffective.[23]

In 1988 the UK Parliament passed a new Merchant Shipping Act. It was framed to deal with the problem of quota hopping. It restricted registration of fishing vessels under the British flag to ships owned or controlled by British individuals or British-owned companies. The mere registration of a company in Britain was no longer sufficient.

Factortame Limited and other Spanish-owned companies challenged the validity of the 1988 Act and the rules made under it. The European Court ruled[24] that they were not compatible with Article 52 (now 43) of the Treaty of Rome, which provides for the freedom of establishment of individuals in other member-states. This led to the amendment of the invalid Merchant Shipping Act to bring it into conformity with Community law as pronounced by the ECJ. But this was not the end of the matter. The Spanish fishermen launched claims for compensation for the period during which they had been prevented from fishing against the British quota, and the validity of these claims for compensation has been

---

23   See *R v. MAFF, Ex p. Agegate*, Case 3/87.
24   Case C-221/89, [1991] 3 CMLR 589.

upheld by the ECJ.[25] Similarly, in other fields such as those of sex discrimination and the environment, the British legal system has acted as a vehicle for the enforcement of Community law.

However, it cannot simply be assumed that the situation is symmetrical in all member-states or that British individuals or businesses would in parallel circumstances be as successful in securing the enforcement of rights theoretically laid down by Community law. The legal systems of Northern European states such as Germany are probably of comparable effectiveness in permitting the enforcement of Community rights but the same may not be true of all other member-states. For example, France has a judicial tradition of upholding the interests of the French state.[26] And although evidence can only be anecdotal, it is far from clear that the legal systems of Southern European countries are as effective as those of Northern Europe.

In conclusion, it must be questioned whether the direct effect of Community law via national legal systems is of net benefit to the economic interests of the UK. The strong and transparent nature of the legal systems in the constituent parts of the UK means that Community rules, as interpreted by the European Court, are enforceable at the suit of affected individuals and businesses. However, differences in the effectiveness of national legal systems mean that there is asymmetry in the strength of enforcement: the rules are more strongly enforced within and against the UK than in some other member-states. This asymmetry may itself lead to a

---

25 *Brasserie du Pecheur v. Germany/R v. Sec of State for Transport ex p. Factortame,* Joined Cases C-46/93 and C-48/93, 7 March 1996.

26 The case of *Minister of Interior v. Cohn-Bendit* [1980] 1 CMLR 543 is a good illustration, where the French Conseil d'État ignored a directly relevant decision of the ECJ in upholding a decision to deport an individual from France on political grounds.

net disbenefit to the UK as compared with a situation where the rules were only enforced at international level and therefore probably less effectively against all parties.

Moreover, Community rules are interpreted with other objectives in mind than the promotion of free trade, such as social or environmental objectives, which have led to demonstrable costs.[27] If there were evidence that, for example, British companies were successfully suing in the French courts for breaches of the EC Public Procurement Directive by French public authorities, there would be a basis for saying that the direct effect of Community law in the context of the single-market rules may produce net positive benefits for the UK. As it is, it is equally possible to claim that the UK suffers a net disbenefit from this aspect of the EC. In view of the unquantifiable nature of the arguments, it is not possible to place this as a concrete item on either the plus or minus side of the ledger.

A comparison of the EC single market and the world trade system after the Uruguay Round
Direct impact on UK exports to EC members

Appendix B sets out the main features of the world trade system after the conclusion of the Uruguay Round of GATT in 1994. That is the baseline this Occasional Paper uses for the purposes of comparison, in order to assess the costs and benefits of belonging to the European Union and hence the EC single market. This baseline – the outside world after the conclusion of the Uruguay Round –

---

27 For example, the costs to UK businesses arising from the *Barber v. Guardian Royal Exchange* Case C-262/88 [1990] 2 CMLR 513, which established the principle of sex equality in pension rights; and the large costs of upgrading water treatment facilities under the water treatment directives.

has important differences from the world trading system which existed when the UK took the decision to join the common market in 1972. How would the position of the UK differ, in terms of access to the EC single market, in today's world if the UK were outside the EC and had no special status or relationship with it?

First, British exports of goods would face the EC's common external customs tariffs and the need to process goods through customs formalities. The tariffs are limited by GATT 1994 and their maximum cost can be calculated (see Chapter 4). Customs rules are a source of cost and delay; however, the internal VAT controls and other formalities involved in trading into the single market following the cessation of customs formalities in 1993 are themselves burdensome.

Second, the UK would cease to be bound by harmonisation directives relating to goods and would be free to set its own standards or indeed no standards at all. Exporters with substantial trade with the EC would, in practice, need to comply with EC standards in order to export to the EC. They might have to have two standards of goods, one for export into the EC and one for the home market, but they might be in this situation anyway if they have an existing third-country export trade.

The UK's ability to influence the content of EC single-market directives would obviously be greatly reduced. To that extent, UK exporters might face future barriers which would not otherwise have existed, if the EC adopts internal standards which do not suit UK exporting producer industries. However, the EC's ability to impose arbitrary, unjustifiable or discriminatory technical standards is now restricted by the two GATT multilateral agreements (outlined in Appendix B) on Sanitary Measures and on Technical Barriers to Trade, as well as in general terms by GATT 1994 itself.

A similar calculus of advantages and disadvantages exists in the case of services. In order to provide services under the umbrella of one of the EC harmonisation directives (for example, insurance services) it is probable that British exporters of services would need to establish branches, subsidiaries or representative offices within the Community. This might make little difference in the case of large-scale trade where such local offices are in practice necessary in any event, but could affect the smaller-scale direct cross-border provision of services. On the plus side, the UK services sector would be free of potentially burdensome EC directives in its servicing of the domestic market and in third-country exports.

There is, in any case, a prospect of long-term liberalisation of trade in the services sector under the framework provided by the General Agreement on Trade in Services (GATS).

State subsidies and public procurement

The UK would no longer be within the EC system for controlling state subsidies, nor within the scope of the EC public procurement directive. The Commission's system of controlling state subsidies has the weakness that it is subject to political influence. The system would of course continue for internal reasons even if the UK were no longer a member, although one would expect there to be less sensitivity to the interests of UK industries which might be adversely affected by state subsidies to industries within the EC. On the other hand, state subsidies are now potentially subject to the GATT disputes procedure under the Agreement on Subsidies and Countervailing Measures. This Agreement, unlike the EC's internal subsidy control system, would apply to subsidies given by the

EC itself, for example as part of its industrial development programme.

Public procurement is the subject of another Uruguay Round agreement, the Agreement on Government Procurement. This, unlike most of the GATT agreements, binds only the countries which have accepted it.[28] This requires non-discrimination against foreign suppliers in public procurement contracts, and public tendering procedures.

Budgetary effects and social and environmental costs

As a non-member of the EC, Britain would not have to contribute to the EC budget. Of course it would lose the benefit of EC programmes which involve spending inside the UK. However, there would be a pure saving of the net contribution and in addition the UK would be able to replace EC spending programmes within the UK in accordance with its own priorities.

The cost imposed on British industry by EC social rules would be capable of being removed. Clearly, there would be a policy choice as to the extent that EC rules on, say, limitations on working time and holiday and leave entitlements would be continued as rules of national origin. A similar calculus would apply to environmental costs; but there would clearly be a better prospect of ending rules which are of little environmental benefit but impose large costs.

---

28   Marrakesh Agreement, Article II(3).

Agriculture and fisheries

Agriculture would obviously be greatly affected since Britain would exit from the Common Agricultural Policy. Presumably there would be some nationally based agricultural support policy, whether on a transitional or permanent basis. The policy would need to stay within the subsidy restrictions imposed by the GATT Agreement on Agriculture, but this is unlikely to be a restraint on a national UK food policy which would most likely be more consumer oriented than the CAP. Thus, one could foresee significant savings for the British taxpayer and consumer.

In the absence of EC membership, the fisheries rights of the UK would revert to those prevailing under general international law. This confers a general exclusive right over fishing in the economic zone surrounding the UK, whose boundaries would *prima facie* conform to those agreed or determined for the UK's continental shelf mineral exploitation rights. On any view, and even though some species of fish migrate across boundary lines, this is likely to be substantially more favourable for the British fishing industry than the Common Fisheries Policy. The impact on consumers of fish is difficult to assess, since it would depend very much on the nature of the national fisheries régime which would follow, and to what extent fish could be landed at British and continental ports.

3 POSSIBLE ALTERNATIVES TO EU MEMBERSHIP

The alternatives: a critique

So far, our baseline for comparison has been the state of affairs which would exist if the UK ceased to be a member of the European Union and had no continuing special relationship or connection with it. However, in between that and full membership are a number of possible alternatives. These differ in terms of degree of access to the European single market, but differ inversely in terms of increased independence of action by the UK and its businesses.

European Economic Area membership

The European Economic Area (EEA) is now of little economic importance, but continues to have possible value as a precedent for a treaty structure.[1]

The main features of the EEA are, first, that it is a free trade area rather than a customs union; hence its members retain responsibility for setting their own tariffs with countries outside the area and may enter into special trading relationships with third countries. This is a freedom denied to members of the EC, which is

---

1 Following the accession of Sweden, Finland and Austria to the European Union, only Norway and Iceland are now EEA members, while Switzerland remains associated with the EC single market through the European Free Trade Area (EFTA).

a full customs union. Second, EEA members enjoy in full the 'four freedoms' of the European single market: freedom of movement of goods, of services, of persons and of capital. Apart from certain supranational activities undertaken by a competition authority, the EEA agreement does not require direct applicability of its provisions within the legal systems of its member-states in the same way as Community law. Furthermore, the EEA leaves agriculture and fisheries as matters of purely national responsibility.

The main defect of the EEA is that it is institutionally biased. The EEA states are obliged to implement the existing body of EC single-market harmonisation measures.[2] EEA states are not compelled to implement future EC single-market directives but, if they fail to do so, the benefits of the agreement may cease to apply to the sector concerned; in other words, trade in that sector between the EC and the EEA country which refuses to implement the directive reverts to multilateral GATT (General Agreement on Tariffs and Trade) rules, involving tariffs if relevant. EEA members have a right to be consulted on, but do not have a vote on the form of, those future directives. There is a complicated mechanism by which they are strongly encouraged, if not compelled, to follow decisions of the European Court on the interpretation of single-market rules.

Thus, EEA membership would do little to ease the present regulatory burden attached to the single market if that were thought to be one of the main drawbacks of full EU membership. However, the flexibility in the adoption of future directives can be considered a potential advantage. Even though the price of refusal to implement an EC directive is that the industry then falls outside the

---

2   The *list* of single-market directives and measures which the EEA members are required to implement, which is annexed to the EEA Agreement, runs to several hundred pages. The measures themselves cover many thousands of pages.

free trade rules of the EEA agreement, there might be instances where that would be an advantage if a directive were perceived as particularly onerous to the UK industry concerned. The UK industry would not thereby be excluded from the EC market: its access to the market would simply then fall under multilateral or GATT rules, which might not make much difference. The ability which the EEA provides to 'pick and choose' future items of single-market legislation means that this arrangement should not be rejected out of hand.

So the EEA can be considered as having considerable attractions in its substantive terms; but it is unattractive institutionally since it would leave the UK closely tied to the single market while limiting its ability to influence single-market rules. It would do little to free British industry of the existing regulatory burden imposed by single-market harmonisation directives, but could increase future flexibility.

Outer-tier Community membership

The institutional unfairness of the EEA arose from the weak bargaining position of the EEA members. It might therefore be possible to correct its defects. Within the EC, an institutional precedent was created which could be adapted for this purpose: the Protocol on Social Policy provided for the institutions of the Community to be used to service the Agreement on Social Policy, to which all member-states belonged except the UK. The UK could not vote in the Council of Ministers on measures taken under the Social Agreement but could fully participate in, and vote on, matters arising under the Rome Treaty to which it belonged.

The same institutional arrangement could be used, but with

the substantive treaty arrangements being modelled on the EEA. Thus, outer-tier Community members would adhere to those aspects of the Rome Treaty (and associated regulations and directives) which pertain to the single market and its four freedoms. They would retain full rights to vote on those matters, and free-trading rules would continue to be binding on all member-states, both inner and outer tier. In the same way as they now do under the Social Agreement, inner-tier members alone would vote on matters arising under treaty provisions to which they alone belonged. They would be free to develop further the process of constructing a European state if that were their wish.

In such a structure, it would be desirable to achieve clear and effective separation between the policy fields which continue to be covered by the outer-tier free trade parts of the treaty, and the treaty aspects which relate to the inner tier. The main problem, for example, with the Maastricht Treaty's social policy opt-out (abandoned in 1997 by the incoming Labour Government) was that it excluded the UK only from an ill-defined part of the social policy field, leaving it directly affected by other aspects of social policy under the Treaty of Rome and the Single European Act.[3]

This type of problem could be overcome by pressing for total separation of outer-tier members from complete policy areas covered by inner-tier treaty provisions.

The European Commission itself could readily be divided, along the lines of existing Directorates-General, into a common market authority (covering internal market, competition and state aids) and a separate inner-tier Commission covering inner-core

---

3   The consequences of this arrangement are dealt with more fully by Martin Howe
     in *Maastricht and 'Social Europe': An escape or an entrapment?*, Oxford, Nelson &
     Pollard, 1993.

matters. This would help to provide a further fire wall against excessive influence by inner-core members on outer-tier matters.

There are other important areas where exclusion from participating in the inner tier would be of benefit to Britain. There is strong pressure under existing treaty arrangements for Britain to participate in a whole range of harmonisation measures which are said to be linked to the single market. For example, it is argued that the free movement of persons and goods within the single market implies a need to harmonise passport checks and rules relating to the immigration of persons across the EU's external borders, as well as criminal justice and even substantive criminal law. Even though an opt-out attached to the Amsterdam Treaty gave Britain the right to exclude itself from certain areas of such measures, the pressure to conform with EU-wide measures in such areas remains strong under existing Treaty structures.

However, the facts of geography mean that the Channel is a natural place to exercise passport controls, and there are serious potential disadvantages in giving this up in order to rely on an imperfect common EU system of immigration control, particularly since the UK's own power to exercise controls on arrivals from third countries would be restricted by its obligations under the common external system and by decisions of the European Court. An EEA-type treaty arrangement, or an EC outer-tier arrangement modelled on the EEA, would exclude the UK from a common EU passport checking system, while retaining the substantive freedoms of movement of British citizens in Europe and of EU citizens here.

Looser forms of relationship

The EC has a variety of forms of free-trading relationship with different categories of non-member-states. These include East European ex-communist countries, southern and eastern Mediterranean countries, and special relationships with developing countries. However, the most relevant relationship for present purposes is that between the EC and Switzerland which derives from the original European Free Trade Area of which Britain was a member before she joined the EC.

When Britain joined the EEC in 1973 (together with Denmark and Ireland), its existing free-trade links with other EFTA members were replaced with free-trade agreements between them and the Community as a whole. The essence of those agreements is tariff-free trade in goods.[4]

The distinction between a customs union (such as the EC) and a free trade area is that within a free trade area the free trade applies only to goods originating in the area, and not to goods imported from outside. Members of the free trade area may have differing external tariffs which could be avoided by trans-shipping goods through the country with lowest tariffs; so customs formalities are exercised on trade between members of the area and 'rules of origin' are applied to determine whether or not the goods concerned are entitled to free entry. Since it is necessary to prevent avoidance of customs dues through minor repackaging or representations of goods originating outside the free trade area, the rules of origin become quite complex.

On the other hand, a customs union requires that all its

---

4   Agreement of 22 July 1972 between the European Economic Community and the Swiss Confederation, Article 3. There are similar agreements between the EC and the other EFTA countries.

members maintain a single external system of tariffs and (if imposed) quotas. Thus, members of a customs union lose the ability to forge their own relationships with other parties. It is, for instance, in principle possible for a country to be a member of two different free trade areas; but it is not possible for a country to belong to two different customs unions.

In fact, the practicalities of belonging to more than one free trade area or agreement within Europe have been greatly eased by the development of the Pan-European Cumulation System.[5] This involved the adoption by the four EFTA countries and the ten Central and Eastern European countries linked to them by a patchwork of free-trade agreements, of a common system of rules of origin, so reducing the administrative burdens of belonging to different free-trade arrangements which would arise if their rules of origin differed from each other. Basically, rules of origin require that a certain amount of processing or work is done on the goods within the free trade area before they count as originating within the area. The second aspect of the Pan-European System is that processing or work on goods done anywhere within the zone counts towards satisfying the rules of origin, so allowing manufacturers to source components and materials from anywhere within the zone without fear of losing free-trade status of their own finished goods anywhere in the zone.

The EEC/Switzerland free-trade agreement established a free trade area between Switzerland and the EEC by providing for the abolition of tariffs and other measures having similar effect on non-agricultural goods originating in Switzerland and the EEC re-

---

5   This system is outlined by Ronald Stewart-Brown, *Global Britain Briefing Note* No. 11, 21 January 2001.

spectively.[6] Rules are laid down to decide what goods count as originating within the free trade area: essentially these are goods which are either wholly manufactured within the area, or which are based on imported goods but have undergone 'sufficient working or processing'.[7] In terminology similar to that of Articles 28 to 30 of the Treaty of Rome, the agreement prohibits quantitative restrictions or measures having equivalent effect on trade between Switzerland and the EEC.[8] It requires that health and safety and technical standards, and other internal measures, shall be non-discriminatory in both the agricultural[9] and non-agricultural[10] sectors.

If the UK were to leave the European Union, a free-trade agreement with the EC on the Swiss/EFTA model would have considerable attractions. It would not inhibit the UK's ability to forge special links with third countries, such as with North America.[11] It would provide tariff-free access for non-agricultural goods to the EC single market: the difference from the present arrangements would be in terms of customs formalities.

A possible variation on such a basic EFTA-style free-trade relationship might be to negotiate 'home country' certification and regulation agreements covering goods and services in areas where existing single-market directives have brought about a harmonisation of standards. There would be a considerable mutual interest between the remaining EU members and a departing Britain to

---

6   EEC/Swiss Agreement, Article 2.

7   *Ibid.*, Protocol 3. The detailed rules laid down are quite complex.

8   *Ibid.*, Articles 13, 13A and 20.

9   *Ibid.*, Article 15(2).

10   *Ibid.*, Article 18.

11   In 2000, Mexico concluded a free-trade agreement with the EC, demonstrating the practicality of a country belonging both to a free-trade arrangement with the EC and to NAFTA simultaneously.

negotiate such arrangements in order to preserve existing trading patterns. If such an arrangement were to be negotiated, it would diminish one of the serious practical problems which would affect British exporters to the EU (and EU exporters to Britain) following a withdrawal from full membership.

The motivation for the EC to enter into a free-trade relationship with a departing Britain would be self-interest, not charity. Given the trade in goods between the UK and other EC members, and the fact that such trade has now taken place on a tariff-free basis for 28 years, it would not be in the EC's interest to disrupt that trade by erecting unnecessary barriers. Some form of relationship along these lines may therefore be a more realistic alternative to European Union membership than our baseline 'worst case' in which the UK becomes a completely free-standing member of the world trading system. If an EFTA-type relationship is considered as a viable alternative, the cost of tariffs on exports to the EC should be deleted from the 'benefits' side of the ledger arising from EU membership.

Mechanisms of withdrawal from the European Union

Given the doctrine of the supremacy of European Community law, an important issue is whether Britain would have the power to leave the European Union, should it wish to do so. Uncertainty over this issue arises from the failure to include any explicit secession or renunciation clauses within the Rome or Maastricht Treaties. It is therefore open to debate whether or not by implication those treaties allow secession on reasonable notice. This legal question could ultimately be decided by the European Court.

However, the fundamental point is that the UK is (in the terminology used by international lawyers) not a 'monist' but a 'dualist' country. This means that international law is regarded by Britain's internal law as a separate system of law; international treaties do not give rise to legal rights or obligations enforceable before British courts of law, subject to a number of limited exceptions not relevant for present purposes.

In consequence, regardless of the question of treaty interpretation, it is clear that Britain does possess the effective legal power to secede, because Parliament could terminate the enforceability of Community law in the British courts. Community law has force and is recognised in British courts solely through the will of Parliament, as expressed in Section 2(1) of the European Communities Act 1972. The courts have held that Community law strikes down Acts of Parliament which conflict with it but their approach is one of divining the intention of Parliament as expressed in the later Act. If the later Act says nothing expressly about conflicts with Community law, then it is to be interpreted as if a section were written into it, saying that its provisions were to be subject to Community law as given effect by the 1972 Act.[12] The consequence is that if Parliament does make it expressly clear, by stating that a new Act is to prevail over s. 2(1) of the European Communities Act 1972 and so prevail over Community law deriving force hereunder, then the new Act will prevail as part of the law of the UK.[13]

12 See Lord Bridge in *R. v. Secretary of State for Transport ex p. Factortame Ltd* [1990] 2 AC 85 at 140B-D.

13 This approach is further reinforced since the House of Lords held in *Pepper v. Hart* that the courts are entitled to look at *Hansard* to resolve ambiguities. In speaking on the 1972 Act which he had drafted, the then Solicitor-General, Sir Geoffrey Howe (now Lord Howe), expressly stated that the Act would not affect the ultimate supremacy of Parliament: *Hansard*, 5th series, p. 838, col. 1319. A similar statement was made by Geoffrey Rippon, proposer of the Bill, during the second reading debate: 15 February 1972, col. 278–9.

In practice, it is far more likely that a withdrawal would take place by agreement rather than by a messy unilateral break. It is hard to see what incentive other member-states would have to restrain a reluctant member from leaving, thus causing endless trouble by compelling it to stay. The economic benefits to the European Union of an orderly reconfiguration of the relationship would be as great as, or greater than, those to the UK. Scenarios of conflict arising from a unilateral termination are probably not realistic. Nevertheless, the analysis of the legal position set out above is of value in illustrating that the UK is not in a position where it would be forced to pay a premium or 'blackmail' price in return for permission to leave if it were to decide to take that step.

4 ECONOMIC COSTS AND BENEFITS OF WITHDRAWAL

The economic costs and benefits to Britain of withdrawal from the EU[1] depend upon the legal framework that would control relations between the UK and the EU after withdrawal. We suggest later in this chapter that a free-trade arrangement would be negotiable. For present purposes, though, it seems best to concentrate on the case in which, after withdrawal, there is no special relation between the EU and the UK.

One reason is caution: no one knows what the position would be after withdrawal, so caution dictates a focus on the situation that many will regard as the worst case. The cry that it would be economic suicide for Britain to leave the EU provides a second reason. A focus on withdrawal without any ensuing special relationship with the EU allows that argument to be tested to the full.

The evidence does not favour the suicide proposition. Many of the world's most successful economies are small and lack favoured access to large markets. Even putting such indirect evidence to one side, however, the plausibility of the notion that Britain would suffer enormous economic costs as a consequence of leaving the EU can be assessed without sophisticated economic calculation, merely by inspecting some relevant magnitudes.

---

1   In Chapters 4 and 5 and Appendix A, for simplicity the generic term 'European Union' or 'EU' is used, even if, strictly speaking, it is the European Community (EC) which is under discussion. Differences between the EU and the EC are explained on pages 46–7.

Table 1 **Selected magnitudes relevant to UK membership of the EU, 1998**

Selected magnitudes, 1998	Percentage of GDP
Household expenditure on food	6.4[a]
Exports of goods to other EU members	11.3[b]
Exports of goods outside the EU	8.1[c]
Exports of services to other EU members	2.5[d]
Exports of services outside the EU	4.6[e]
Earnings of UK-owned assets in the EU	5.3[f]
Earnings of UK-owned assets in the rest of the world	7.9[f]
Directly owned foreign capital in the UK	24.4[g]
Foreign direct investment in the UK	4.8[h]
UK gross capital formation (excluding dwellings)	18.0[i]
UK gross contribution to the EU budget	1.2[j]

a   ONS, *Annual Abstract of Statistics 2000* (AAS) p. 248

b   AAS p. 306

c   ONS, *UK Balance of Payments: The Pink Book*, 1999 (PB) p. 130

d   PB p. 130

e   PB p. 82

f   United Nations, *World Investment Report 2000*, p. 283

g   PB, p. 96

h   PB, p. 78

i   AAS p. 310

j   PB, p. 138

Putting the EU into perspective

The most important of these magnitudes are given in Table 1 above. They clearly indicate that detailed assessment of the costs or benefits of EU membership is unlikely to yield large numbers, relative to British GDP. This applies to both negative and positive features of Britain's relationship with the EU.

The Common Agricultural Policy

Casual observation, for example, suggests that the CAP creates large distortions and is likely to be a very expensive policy. More detailed examination confirms that casual observation is correct, and, if anything, conservative.

But food accounts for only 6.4 per cent of GDP; and the losses of British consumers and taxpayers are offset by the gains from the CAP of British landowners. Even the very large distortions of the CAP, therefore, are unlikely to create losses that are a large fraction of GDP.

The calculations reported in Appendix A, Section 1, indicate that the net cost of the CAP to Britain was about £4.5 billion in 1998. This is lower than the figure calculated on the same basis for 1994, which was £6.4 billion: the estimated costs of the CAP to British consumers and taxpayers have fallen by £1.3 billion and estimated payments to British farmers have risen by £0.6 billion. Expressed as a percentage of GDP, the estimated cost of the CAP is just over half of 1 per cent of GDP. Appendix A suggests that this is an underestimate. Nevertheless, a figure of very much more than 1 per cent of GDP for the net welfare loss from the CAP for 1998 might be difficult to defend.[2]

Withdrawal from the EU would mean escape from the CAP. That would lead to an economic gain, and a substantial one, though less than some of the wilder figures put about.

Other elements in the balance, however, run in the opposite di-

---

2   Borrell, Brent and Lionel Hubbard, 2000, 'Global economic effects of the EU Common Agricultural Policy', *Economic Affairs*, Vol 20, No.2 (June 2000) pp. 18–26. The authors (p. 21) however, comment, on the basis of much more sophisticated calculations than those given in Appendix A, that 'The total cost to the world economy [of the CAP] is US$75 billion a year. Two-thirds of this is borne by the EU itself: US$49 billion a year, or around 0.8 per cent of GDP'. No calculation for the UK is given, but losses for the UK, with its relatively small farming population, are likely to be greater, relative to GDP, than for the EU as a whole. The tables in Borrell and Hubbard suggest that their discussion is based on 1998 figures, but this is not explicitly stated.

rection. Do they exceed the loss from the CAP? More important, do they provide support for the withdrawal-is-economic-suicide school?

Visible trade

Can the 11. 3 per cent of GDP represented by visible exports to the EU play that role, for example? A loss of markets of that magnitude would be accompanied by substantial economic disruption.

But UK withdrawal from the EU is not tantamount to cessation of trade with the EU. If Britain left the EU without negotiating any special arrangement for trade, the EU would impose its 'most-favoured-nation' tariff (the highest permissible under the rules of the WTO [World Trade Organisation]) on exports from Britain. That is a relatively low tariff – perhaps, properly averaged, around 6 per cent.[3] The maximum cost to the British economy would occur if British exporters held their prices to EU buyers constant, and paid the re-imposed EU import duties out of their revenues. So the *maximum* economic loss on this item, in the worst possible case, is $0.113 \times 0.06 = 0.00678$ of GDP: less than three-quarters of 1 per cent of GDP.

The actual loss would be smaller. Economic adjustment brought about by changes in prices and exchange rates would increase sales outside the EU. Such switching of destinations would reduce the cost to Britain of EU tariffs. Of course, the adjustment might require declines in labour costs. Disruption from that source, however, would be countered by the cheaper food that escape from the CAP makes possible.

---

3   Appendix A discusses different methods of obtaining an average EU tariff and explains how the 6 per cent figure is arrived at.

This is a very different picture from the one sometimes presented. The notion that 'Britain has no economic future outside the EU' gains its force from the idea that Britain would be shut out of the EU market if it left the EU. But there is no basis in fact or law for such a supposition. 'Britain has no economic future outside the EU' is no more than silly, windy rhetoric.

Effects of customs unions on international trade

A major reason for such concerns lies in a simple error. The EU is in part a customs union. It aims for free trade between members, but maintains barriers against imports from non-members – hence, trade between members is encouraged and trade with the rest of the world discouraged. This concentration of trade between members, however, is not evidence that the customs union has had beneficial consequences: only of its existence.

The concentration of trade caused by the customs union is often cited to support the case that the EU brings economic benefits to the UK. Lord Howe, for example, writing in the *Financial Times* (7 August 1996), comments that 'Since 1973, UK exports to EU states have grown twice as rapidly as to the rest of the world. Visible exports to Germany alone now equal those to the US and Japan combined.' Observations like this are frequently left to stand without further comment, as though their significance were self-evident. But it is not.

Had Britain entered a customs union with the United States in 1973, British trade would have been biased towards the US (instead of *against* the US, which has been the effect of EU membership). Calculations made in 1996 would have shown that British trade with the US had grown faster than British trade with other countries, and Lord Howe might have written articles congratulating Britain on its choice of the US as its favoured trading partner. But the more rapid growth of trade with partners in a customs union merely reflects the existence of the union.[4] It says nothing about the fitness of the union or the economic benefits that derive from it.

Similarly, had Britain entered a customs union with the United States in 1973, the bias of customs unions probably would have made the US a larger customer than Germany and Japan combined. (In 1998, the US imported more British goods than Germany, even though British exports to the US were subject to tariffs). But that would be poor evidence for a claim that the hypothetical US–UK union was economically beneficial.

Simple observation of the pattern of trade does not carry great weight in discussion of the economic merits of belonging to the EU. What weight it has relates to the adjustment entailed in leaving the EU. If virtually all British exports went to the EU, concern that the British economy was in some sense dependent on EU protection, and that it would be dangerous and costly to step outside that magic circle, would be understandable.

But that is not the situation. Many British exports now go to destinations outside the EU: almost half of British visible exports in terms of value, and well over half of invisible exports (discussed separately below). That half of British exports go outside the EU suggests that the ability to export of British industry does not de-

---

4   There is no presumption, though, that trade with customs-union partners will grow faster than trade with outsiders once adjustment to the union is complete. The presumption that it will grow faster requires inclusion of the period at the start of the union. Lord Howe, measuring from 1973, includes the period of adjustment between Britain and the EU.

pend upon the absence of tariffs on British exports to the EU, nor upon any other special features of access to the European single market. It suggests that adjusting to life outside the EU, which would in part entail selling more goods to the rest of the world, is perfectly feasible and not dangerously costly. Examination of Table 3 of Appendix A, which provides details of trade in different products, confirms this.

In trade terms, moreover, leaving the EU would yield benefits as well as costs. As noted above, customs unions create artificial incentives to buy the products of fellow members, rather than the cheaper products of non-members. Dutch and US widgets might both sell in Britain for £10. If Dutch widgets enter duty free, because there is a customs union between Britain and the Netherlands, while American widgets pay a £3 import duty, the British government loses £3 of tariff revenue every time a Dutch widget is purchased rather than an American one. No gain offsets that loss.[5]

Foreign Direct Investment

Foreign direct investment (FDI) in Britain is high on the list of arguments suggesting that it would be disastrous to leave the EU.

---

5   Some seem to think that an offsetting gain appears if British purchases of high-price widgets from the Dutch allow the British to sell the Dutch something at £20 that the Dutch could get from Australia at £15. Would that it were so easy to become prosperous! The butcher, the baker and the candle-stick maker could then become rich by agreeing to buy one another's wares at higher than market prices.

They cannot become rich by that means, of course. A gain to one is a loss to others, so that while one might gain, not all can. All can lose, however. The high-price agreement gives each an incentive to economise unduly on the high-price goods imported from their partners. The parties to the agreement will therefore be worse off, in aggregate, than if there were no agreement.

Inward FDI would dry up, the argument runs, and the economy would suffer great harm.

The hypothesis that the flow of FDI would cease if Britain left the EU is based on a second hypothesis, often left implicit. This is that Britain is an attractive location for foreign investors *only* because Britain offers access to markets in the rest of the EU. So baldly stated, however, this notion is not tenable.

Any other location in the EU also offers access to EU markets. Access to the EU therefore cannot explain why so many inward investors choose Britain instead of alternative EU locations. The fact that they do choose Britain suggests that a British location offers advantages over and above other EU locations – over and above, in other words, access to the EU.

Moreover, companies based in other member-states invest in Britain (Table 4 in Appendix A gives figures). Clearly, such investment cannot be explained in terms of access to EU markets.

Two specific advantages of investing in Britain are often cited. One is the English language and the other is Britain's relatively de-regulated labour market. But while the English language perhaps might explain why companies from Japan or Korea invest in Britain, it is a much less plausible explanation of investment by French or German companies, and totally implausible as an explanation of Irish FDI. The prominent presence of these countries in the list of FDI in Britain suggests that the deregulated labour market is the dominant consideration.

Regardless of which attraction is the more important for foreign investors, neither will vanish as a consequence of Britain leaving the EU. Indeed, departure from the EU would leave Britain freer to determine its labour market policies. The scope and cost to employers of EU laws relating to the labour market has grown and grown. The original provisions of the Rome Treaty on equal pay, and sex discrimination directives dating from the 1970s, have been repeatedly reinterpreted, always expanding their scope. Their scope of application has been progressively expanded, for example, to require part-time workers to enjoy the full panoply of benefits and security of employment rights as full-time workers. The adherence in 1997 of Britain's Labour government to the so-called Social Chapter, and its acceptance of the Working Time Directive, has further expanded the cost of EU employment law. In December 2000, moreover, the EU Charter of Fundamental Rights was adopted at Nice. Its panoply of entrenched 'social rights' will again increase the costs and inflexibilities of the working practices enforced by EU labour market laws, and reduce even further any faint prospect that these laws might be subject to reform or repeal.

Re-imposition of barriers to exports from Britain to the EU might weigh against Britain as a site for foreign direct investors seeking access to the EU market. But it would not *eliminate* Britain as such a site. The relevant question is how potential investors would balance one factor against the others. If inward investors are primarily concerned with economic returns, there is little reason to suppose that withdrawal from the EU would weigh heavily in the balance.

EU tariffs, as already noted, are far from prohibitive. The impact of EU tariffs on the choice of Britain as a location could be overcome by quite small reductions in British wage or non-wage costs of hiring labour – reductions which, as also noted, would be facilitated by the gain in real wages allowed by escape from the CAP. The reduction in the tax burden following elimination of Britain's escape from paying its net budget contributions to the EU could also reduce the costs that fall on businesses located in Britain, making the UK more attractive for foreign investors.

The media in Britain frequently refers to FDI as a 'vote of confidence in the British economy'; and it is indeed difficult to imagine the current flows arriving in the strike-ridden economy of the 1970s. But while votes of confidence are pleasant to receive, so is money; and the vote-of-confidence formulation elides the question of assessing the actual size of the tangible benefits that inward investment brings to Britain.

A reason for caution in assessing those benefits is that the British government pays inward investors. The amounts paid are not publicly available – itself a ground for suspicion. It is clear, however, that substantial amounts are involved. In July, 1996, for example, British newspapers were reporting a decision of LG (formerly Lucky Goldstar), a Korean conglomerate, to place a £1.7 billion electronics plant in Wales.

It was widely reported that LG had been paid £200 million to locate in Britain; which, it was said, was equivalent to about £30,000 per job. That was contrasted with the lower amounts paid to other investors: 'Even for large schemes creating many jobs, few companies secure more than £20,000 a post' [FT 10 July 1996]. A more recent case that has received much publicity is a £40 million grant to Nissan, in Sunderland, which reports associate with '1,300 jobs' (for example, the FT of January 2001) – that is, a subsidy of more than £30,000 per job. Even the £20,000-a-job subsidy, though, amounts to a lot of money.

Payments to inward investors raise the possibility that the recipient of the FDI is worse off as a consequence. The standard counter to this conjecture is that inward investment generates positive externalities – in the form of know-how acquired by other firms in the economy.

There is, however, little evidence for such an effect. Girma, Greenaway and Wakelin comment (p. 20) that 'even after we allow for productivity differences we still find that foreign firms pay on average 5% more than domestic firms. In terms of nationality, we found American firms to have the largest differential and Japanese firms the smallest'. However, 'When we tested for intra-industry spillovers, we found that on average there were no wage and productivity spillovers to domestic firms as a result of foreign presence, whether in levels or growth'.[6]

If there are no spillovers, on average, as Girma et al suggest, the case for subsidies is badly damaged. That result suggests that FDI brings no gain to Britain through this route. What remains is higher wages. But the 5 per cent on wages noted by Girma et al does not make a good investment out of subsidies that pay the costs per job noted earlier.

Any gain to Britain from these sources may be entirely dissipated by the payments that the British government makes to attract investors or to persuade them to stay.

Unsubsidised FDI is a good thing for recipient economies. FDI that is subsidised by the recipient economy may not be. The role of subsidies to FDI in Britain deserves serious thought.

It is difficult to construct a credible argument that FDI generates a net gain of more than 1 per cent of GDP. The foreign-owned stock of capital in Britain is about 25 per cent of GDP, so a gain of 1 per cent of GDP requires the social rate of return on foreign capital to be 4 per cent per annum over and above the private return

---

6   Girma, Greenaway and Wakelin, 2001, *op. cit.*

including subsidies. It is hard to believe that there is a social rate of return of anything like that magnitude.

Moreover, there is no reason to suppose that FDI will cease as a consequence of withdrawal. The cost of withdrawal on this account is therefore likely to be much less than 1 per cent of GDP – and may in fact be the source of a benefit.

Invisible trade

There are few economies to which invisible trade is as important as it is to the British economy. Provision of services accounts for three-quarters of British employment. Credits for invisible items account for more than half of total credits in the balance of payments.

The category 'invisibles' contains three major sub-categories (each of which itself contains numerous sub-categories). The first is revenue from the provision of services – transport, banking and insurance, professional services, and so on. In 1998, credits from the provision of services accounted for 32 per cent of all credits on the invisible account. The second is income from British-owned investments abroad, which provided 59 per cent of credits. The remaining sub-category is 'transfers', which accounts for 8 per cent of credits and is dominated by governmental transactions. The following discussion focuses on 'services' and 'investment income'.

Credits from the EU are compared with credits from the rest of the world in Table 2. It will be seen that the rest of the EU is a much less important destination for British invisible exports than it is for visible exports.

'Services' and 'investment income' raise different issues from

Table 2 **UK credits from different areas: £ million and percentage of category, 1998**

	EU	*Rest of world*
Services	21,380	38,690
	(35.6%)	(64.4%)
Investment income	44,839	66,526
	(40.3%)	(59.7%)

Source: PB, p. 130 (services) and p. 134 (income).

the standpoint of policy. UK investment income is probably not affected by British membership of the EU, whether for better or for worse. It is the smaller category, 'services', that might be affected by withdrawal.

Table 1 suggests that sales of services in the EU are such a small fraction of GDP that withdrawal from the EU could not possibly cause a large welfare loss to the UK. That is probably true, but it would be misleading to arrive at that conclusion merely on the basis that credits from the sale of services in the EU are small.

The problem is that international transactions in services very often require the provider of a service to establish in the country of the receiver of the service. This is discussed in more detail in Appendix A, Section IV. The figure in Table 1, however, is based on sales from British-based service providers only. Sales of the wholly owned subsidiary of a British advertising agency or management consultant in Hong Kong or Paris play no direct role in the determination of that figure (though they may play an indirect role if the subsidiary pays fees to a British-based person). The remitted profits of such agencies will appear in the British accounts as investment income.

That exports of services are a small fraction of GDP therefore does not mean that international transactions in services are not important to the British economy, whether the sales are in the EU or elsewhere. To assess the possible impact of British withdrawal from the EU, it is necessary to take account of the structure of international transactions in services, which typically entails the establishment of foreign subsidiaries.

Appendix A, Section IV attempts to do this. The more correct, but also more complicated route, however, yields the same answer as the figures in Table 1. So far as trade in services is concerned, withdrawal from the EU is unlikely to impose a large economic cost on the UK.

Gains and losses

Trade with the rest of the EU; the CAP; and FDI are the big-ticket items in the debate about the economic costs or benefits of staying in the EU or of leaving it. Between them, they cover a high proportion of the measurable costs and benefits of EU membership.[7]

What is striking, though, is that the economic gains and losses associated with each individual item are small relative to British GDP. Moreover, they offset one another. There is:

(a) a sure gain from leaving the CAP;
(b) a loss from re-imposition of EU tariffs on UK exports to the EU;

---

7   British contributions to the EC budget are measurable, but are not explicitly discussed here. One reason is that the CAP accounts for a large fraction of the budget, so that to discuss the cost of the CAP and the budget could entail double counting. A more important reason, however, is that there is no obvious relationship between budgetary costs and credits and economic costs and benefits. The budgetary cost of ordaining that three-quarters of agricultural land should lie fallow, for example, might be very small. The economic cost, on the other hand, might be very large.

(c) a whole or partial offset to (b) as a consequence of removing the distorting effect of EU tariffs on the sources of imports into the UK; and

(d) a possible loss from a possible reduction in FDI.

The *net* effect, therefore, is small.

The analysis provided here does not allow a confident claim that the British economy would gain from withdrawal. The central point, however, is that any economic gain or loss is small – almost certainly less than 1 per cent of GDP. Even the worst case – a loss of 1 per cent of GDP – is a long way from economic suicide.

The estimates are necessarily approximate. It is the order of magnitude of costs and benefits that we have sought to define, not precise numbers. The estimates strongly suggest, however, that more precise or more sophisticated calculations will not arrive at a large number for either gain or loss. Had the analysis led to a loss of 20 per cent of GDP on one account, and an offsetting gain of 20 per cent on another, different measurements (or correction of errors in measurement) might yield alternative estimates of *net* gain or loss that are substantial relative to GDP. But the orders of magnitude actually observed are less than 1 per cent of GDP. Under that circumstance, the proposition that withdrawal will lead to only small overall economic gains or losses is robust.

The estimates presented here, it should be emphasised, are based on the worst case – an absence of any special relationship covering trade between the EU and a departed Britain. The conclusion of Chapter 3 was that arrangements better than the worst case would most likely be available. The entry of Britain into such arrangements might well therefore lead to net economic benefits, or, at worst, to a very small net economic loss.

Only persons of a hysterical disposition could describe these results in terms of 'economic suicide' or 'economic disaster'. Britain can prosper outside the EU. Whether the British would wish to do so is another question.

5 BETTER OFF OUT?
SOME CONCLUSIONS

To assess the economic costs and benefits of Britain's membership of the European Union, a range of factors must be taken into account. Some are directly measurable (at least in principle) and fairly tangible. Others are less measurable, but still significant.

Tariff barriers and the CAP

Were Britain to leave the European Union (and not enter into one of the alternative relationships with it discussed in Chapter 3), British visible exports to the EU would face tariffs and the CAP would no longer rule in Britain. We estimate that the cost of the tariffs on present trade patterns (using 1998 as a base) will not exceed £5.7 billion, and that the gain from leaving the CAP will be at least £4.5 billion. There might therefore be a loss on these two items together, though, since our estimate of the cost of tariffs is an upper bound, while our estimate of the cost of the CAP is a lower bound, that is not certain.

Of course, British trade patterns would change if Britain was no longer a member of the EU. British exports to the EU of goods bearing high tariffs when exported to the EU would suffer, but compensation for such losses would appear in the form of larger exports to third countries; probably by an expansion of exports to the EU of goods bearing low EU tariffs; and in a new-found ability of British buyers to purchase wherever in the world goods are cheapest, without the distortion of choice created by EU tariffs. These changes of trading patterns would reflect new trading opportunities, and would progressively reduce the cost to British exporters – and the British economy – of the tariffs on exports to the EU.

Non-tariff barriers to trade

Although the cost of tariffs taken by itself is containable and is indeed more than offset by other factors, it is also necessary to take into account the impact of measures other than tariffs on Britain's visible and invisible exports to the EU. Visible exports would face customs formalities. British exporters are, of necessity, currently well adapted to single-market regulations such as products standards, but (in the absence of any negotiated special arrangement) if Britain left the EU, its goods would no longer benefit from recognition of home-country certification where this is relevant. Thus, additional costs would be incurred in obtaining certifications and approvals within the EU.

In the context of services, British exporters could face additional barriers in that they would no longer benefit from rights of establishment conferred by the Treaty of Rome in fields where there are relevant directives, mutual recognition of professional qualifications, or the right to provide services direct from offices in Britain on the basis of home-country regulation. This would not have a major impact in fields where it is in any event necessary for economic or practical reasons to establish branches or subsidiaries in countries to which services are marketed. But it could inhibit trade in fields where the direct provision of services is of economic importance.

These costs, whilst real, are extremely hard to quantify. But off-setting gains would arise from leaving the EU. British industry, whether providing goods or services, would no longer be subject in its domestic market to excessive or unnecessary costs of EU regulations. The extent to which leaving the EU would result in a cost saving under this heading would of course depend upon the policy choices made by the British Government after leaving – in particular, the extent to which it engaged in a bonfire of existing EU regulations.

Measurement of the costs and benefits in this area (benefits of single-market access versus costs of European regulation) is extremely difficult, both in principle and in practice. Only a detailed sector-by-sector survey of individual industries, their dependence on single-market membership for access to the EU market, and the impact on them of European regulations, could hope to present such a picture. But even in such an exercise, it would be necessary to make assumptions (for example, about the non-EU level or nature of regulation which would be appropriate if the UK were to leave) which would be open to debate and discussion, before a baseline against which to measure the costs could be constructed.

Despite these difficulties of quantification, a general point can be made: on the assumption that single-market regulations produce a benefit in terms of easier access to the EU single market, this benefit accrues to only about 14 per cent of the British economy – 12 per cent consisting of visible exports to the EU and 2 per cent consisting of exports of services there. On the other hand, the cost of single-market regulations falls upon up to 100 per cent of the British economy. In crude terms, in order for these less tangible elements of the single market to produce a net benefit to the British economy, it is necessary for the benefits of market access in the industries which benefit from it to be, in percentage terms, about *seven times* as great as the costs of regulation of European origin falling on British industry as a whole. This seems a demanding target. There must be serious doubt whether it can be achieved.

Other economic costs of EU membership

The intangible (but real) economic costs of membership of the EU do not end with the costs associated with the single market (including the CAP) itself. Costs to the British economy arise from European social laws, from the fact that the component of the British EU budget contribution which is spent inside Britain can only be spent according to EU rather than national priorities, and from other European areas of policy such as the environment.

The problem with measuring the net cost of these aspects of EU membership is that they involve either transfer payments or intangible benefits arising from the operation of the policy. Thus, European sex discrimination laws impose costs on employers, but give benefits to, say, part-time workers.[1] The cost to the British economy cannot simply be measured by taking the cost to employers and ignoring the benefit to employees; however, most commentators agree there are real and significant costs imposed by this kind of measure in terms of loss of flexibility and competitiveness.

Similarly, in environmental policy, European laws which prevent the construction of marinas on wetlands occupied by wading birds impose economic costs but, at least in the view of some, con-

---

[1] Because statistically there is a higher proportion of female part-time workers than full-time workers, it can be 'indirect discrimination' contrary to European social laws to discriminate in pay, fringe benefits or statutory employment protection rights between full-time and part-time workers: *R. v. Sec of State for Employment, ex p. Seymour-Smith*, Court of Appeal, *The Times*, 3 August 1995.

fer intangible benefits. How can the costs be measured against the benefits? The lack of national flexibility – the power to set priorities and to weigh the costs against the benefits according to Britain's own national priorities rather than externally imposed priorities – can itself be regarded as a significant cost.

In public expenditure, a substantial proportion of the UK's Community budget contribution is returned and expended within the UK. In one sense, this element of the budget contribution does not 'cost' anything since the net recipients in the UK (the beneficiaries of EU regional policy grants) gain what the British taxpayer loses. However, there is a cost in the sense that these economic resources are not allocated in accordance with national priorities, and hence on that view are misallocated.

All the costs identified above are difficult to measure, but nonetheless real. Moreover, their trend seems to be upwards.

Consequential effects of primary costs and benefits

Some important consequences of EU membership or non-membership, such as foreign direct investment (FDI), depend upon the primary costs and benefits to British industry. Thus, at first sight, the imposition of tariffs on British exports to the EU would be likely to deter FDI in Britain. But that disadvantage could be offset by reductions in labour costs following a policy of cheaper food, by changed social laws, and by lower levels of taxation. The behaviour of decision-makers would depend both on reality and on perceptions as to the benefits and costs of locating in Britain. But if the reality was that British industry received a net benefit following departure from the EU, the perceptions of investors would not be far behind.

Similarly, intangible benefits such as 'market integration' – for example, concentrating manufacturing facilities in one or a few countries – depend upon the effect of the primary costs and benefits. Although tariffs and other barriers would *prima facie* deter companies from locating integrated facilities in the UK in order to serve other EU countries, that *prima facie* deterrence would be overcome if location of facilities in Britain enjoyed net benefits arising from lower costs and more flexible labour practices.

Fears associated with leaving the EU

In thinking about possible 'worst cases', it is useful to consider a further possible argument. It is that the figures are irrelevant because the remaining member-states of the EU will make it their business to impose new costs on a departed Britain. The true costs of departure, this argument continues, will therefore be vastly greater than the analysis offered above suggests.

Would the EU act with deliberate malice towards a departed Britain? What measures would be within its power to take?

It is important to distinguish between the remaining member-states acting towards Britain with deliberate malice and the remaining member-states acting in their own interest. If the UK has no vote in the process of determining EU regulations, EU regulations are likely to be less consistent with UK interests, as compared with a situation in which Britain does have a vote. But that is the position that Britain faces in every other country of the world: it has no vote in the determination of US trade policy, no vote in Japan. The scale of British exports to the rest of the world makes clear, however, that British manufacturers and service providers are quite capable of selling effectively in that situation.

Malice is different. Would the remaining members of the EU go out of their way to act against British interests?

A first point is that, even if it is presumed that our European partners would harbour the necessary depth of malice, activation of it would depend on the manner of a British departure. Broadly speaking, three situations seem possible:

(a) the rest of the EU becomes so exasperated with Britain and its foot dragging that Britain is asked to leave;
(b) the EU develops so far in the direction of unacceptable transfer of sovereignty to a federal state that a British government decides to leave, against the wishes of the other member-states;
(c) each side arrives at the perception that the interests and character of the other are not reconcilable with its own, and agrees, with regret, to separate.

Clearly, (a) and (c) provide fertile ground for the negotiation of arrangements for departure that are beneficial from a British point of view: (b) is more problematic. But (b) also seems extremely improbable. The member-states of the EU could have no interest in seeking to compel another nation to remain part of their venture of European construction against its own will, especially since conscription of such a reluctant country would lead to perpetual arguments and turbulence. Everything therefore suggests that a British departure would be negotiated and orderly. Deliberate EU malice against a departing Britain is not a realistic prognosis: still less is it likely that malice would pointlessly be continued year after year.

What could the EU do?

Still, suppose the EU did wish to act punitively towards a departed Britain. What could it do?

As discussed in Appendix B, the Uruguay Round agreements and the WTO impose significant constraints on the EU's actions with respect to trade. The WTO certainly does not provide complete protection against EU action, but it provides some. For the EU openly to flout WTO disciplines would have a very large negative effect on EU relations with the rest of the world at large, not just with Britain.

Indeed, a departed Britain would have interests with respect to the EU that are similar to those of much of the rest of the world – to the USA, Japan, Australia, Canada and most other countries. The EU would break the fundamental WTO rule if it discriminated against Britain – if it treated exports from Britain differently from similar exports from, say, the United States. To act spitefully against Britain, therefore, the EU would either have to break WTO rules, or act spitefully against the US and other countries as well.

This protection is not absolute. An EU acting maliciously could certainly get away for some considerable time with baseless anti-dumping actions against British exports, for example. That would be irritating and expensive for the British businesses involved – but it would not impose costs at a level that would reverse the earlier conclusions about economic costs and benefits.

What do the economic costs (or benefits) of withdrawal signify?

Members of churches sometimes pay tithes, and it would be absurd to suggest that a member abandon his or her church merely on the basis that the cost of the tithes exceeds the pecuniary benefits of belonging. If being in the EU costs Britain something, that does not mean that Britain should withdraw. If membership of the EU yields economic benefits, that does not mean that Britain should stay. Economic costs and benefits are one aspect of EU membership. No sensible decision to stay or to leave can be made without assessing the value of the other elements.

That value is something on which reasonable and well-intentioned British people differ. Enthusiasts for a European federal structure would, if necessary, pay a great deal to remain members: economic benefits are not central to their position. Some Euro-sceptics would reject membership of a United States of Europe even if the economic benefits of membership could be shown to be very large. That such economic costs as can objectively be assessed are so low strongly suggests that they will not – nor should – weigh heavily in the balance on either side of the argument. The real content of the debate lies elsewhere.

Our analysis, though, leads to rejection of the idea that departure from the EU would have horrific consequences, tantamount to economic suicide. It is in practice hard to tell whether leaving the EU 'cold turkey' would make Britain better or worse off. But the analysis in this Occasional Paper suggests that alternative arrangements with the EU would almost certainly benefit Britain, compared with existing arrangements. The idea that dire economic consequences make UK departure from the EU unthinkable has no evident foundation. If the EU develops along lines that the UK finds unacceptable on fundamental political grounds, fear of adverse economic consequences should not deter a British government from seeking to change the relationship of the UK with the EU, or, in the last resort, from leaving the Union.

APPENDIX A
ECONOMIC ASSESSMENTS

1 THE COMMON AGRICULTURAL POLICY

In 1998, the last year for which figures are currently available, the CAP cost Britain at least £4.5 billion, or just over half of 1 per cent of British GDP. This estimate is based on the work of the Organisation for Economic Cooperation and Development (OECD) which, each year, calculates the costs of its members' agricultural policies, including the cost of the CAP to the EU.[1] The OECD figures can be used to estimate the cost to Britain of the CAP. The figure is therefore well based, but it is almost certainly an underestimate – probably a serious underestimate – of the true cost.

A first useful OECD figure is the burden of the CAP on EU taxpayers (through tax-financed direct support) and consumers (through higher food prices). For 1998, expressed in terms of cost per head of population, this is $362.[2] Converting at an average exchange rate of $1.6570 per pound sterling,[3] this amounts to £218.47 per head. In 1998, the population of the United Kingdom was 59.2 million[4]. Hence, the total cost of the CAP to British tax-

---

1   OECD, 'Agricultural Policies in OECD Countries: Monitoring and Evaluation', 2000.

2   OECD, p. 187.

3   Office of National Statistics, 'Annual Abstract of Statistics 2000' (AAS) p. 398.

4   AAS, p. 26.

payers and food buyers was £12.9 billion.

The value of transfers to EU farmers from EU consumers and taxpayers, expressed as a percentage of the value of farm output was 59.8 per cent in 1998.[5] In that year, the output of British farms was valued at £14 billion[6]. If British farmers received support at the average rate for the EU, therefore, the CAP contributed about £8.4 billion to their income.

The net cost to Britain of the CAP is the difference between the costs the policy imposes on taxpayers and purchasers of food, on the one hand, and the gains of farmers on the other. That net cost is £(12.9 – 8.4) or £4.5 billion.

Sources of error

There are, though, good reasons for believing that this figure *un-der*estimates the true cost of the CAP. The variety of grounds for this belief is discussed below.

Products not included in OECD calculations

First, the OECD figures do not cover the whole range of agricultural products subject to CAP interventions. The OECD figures are calculated for thirteen major agricultural commodities. Excluded from its calculations are fruits and vegetables, potatoes, wine, cotton and tobacco.The OECD itself estimates that its calculations cover 61 per cent of the total value of EU agricultural production.[7]

The products excluded by the OECD are all subject to substan-

---

5   OECD, p. 205.
6   AAS, p. 330.
7   OECD, p. 205.

tial intervention in the EU. In 1994, the share in total price-guarantee expenditures of the EU of fruits and vegetables was 4.8 per cent; of tobacco 3.4 per cent; of 'vine-growing products' 4.3 per cent; and of fibre plants and silk worms 2.5 per cent.[8] There is no reason to suppose that the figures for 1998 are substantially different.

From the UK standpoint, EU expenditure on the production of tobacco, wine and cotton is close to pure cost. UK production of these products is low or non-existent, and is exceeded by far by UK consumption. Hence, there is little offset in the form of enhanced incomes of British producers of these commodities to the costs imposed on British consumers and taxpayers. The OECD figures, therefore, underestimate the cost of the CAP to the UK.

The UK is a substantial producer of fruit and vegetables, and UK producers gain from EU support activities in that area. The UK is also, however, a net importer of fruit and vegetables (to the tune of about £3.8 billion in 1998[9]); so the losses of UK consumers are likely substantially to outweigh the gains of UK horticulturists. Again, therefore, estimates based on OECD figures will underestimate losses to the UK.

True welfare costs

The effects on consumption and use of raised agricultural prices relative to prices in general are not taken into account in the OECD figures, nor the effects of the CAP on the relative prices of different

---

8   Jacob Kol and B. Kuijpers, 'The Cost for Consumers and Taxpayers of the Common Agricultural Policy of the European Union: the case of the Netherlands', Erasmus Papers in International Economic Integration, Erasmus Centre for Economic Integration Studies, Rotterdam, Erasmus University, duplicated, 1996, p. 34.

9   AAS, pp. 304–5.

agricultural commodities. The OECD figures therefore underestimate the cost to consumers of the CAP.

It is sometimes said that the costs of the relative-price distortions brought about by the CAP are small because demand for agricultural products is unresponsive to prices. CAP-created distortions in prices are large, however, so the cost of distortions may be substantial even if elasticities of demand are low.

Effects on world prices

Two situations must be distinguished when discussing the costs to Britain of the CAP. They are:

(a) the EU abandons the CAP and Britain remains a member of the EU; and
(b) the EU maintains the CAP but Britain leaves the EU.

The principal difference between these two situations, in the present context, lies in world prices of agricultural products. The CAP depresses prices in the rest of the world. Were the EU to abandon the CAP [situation (a)], world prices would rise, offsetting (but not eliminating) the benefit that an end to the CAP would bring to EU consumers. If the CAP remained in force when Britain left the EU, however, the depressing effect of the CAP on world prices would continue – and British consumers could buy food at those low prices.

The OECD figures are based on existing world prices. Used in an effort to estimate British gains in situation (a), therefore, they might yield a quite serious overestimate. That source of error is much less serious when considering British gains in situation (b).

British escape from the CAP might increase world prices of agricultural products (depending in part on what the remainder of the EU did with its increased agricultural surpluses). It is unlikely to raise world prices by very much, however. Hence, it is unlikely to be a serious source of overestimation of the costs of the CAP to Britain.

Composition-of-output effects

The estimate above uses OECD averages for the EU as a whole to impute costs and benefits to Britain. That procedure underestimates gains to British farmers if the mix of products produced by British farmers includes more products that are heavily subsidised by the EU than average EU output.

In 1998, the highest percentage subsidy equivalent in the EU was for 'other grains', and amounted to 71 per cent of farm sales of other grains, while eggs received a subsidy equivalent of 10 per cent.[10] A national farming sector that produced a higher percentage of eggs by value than the EU average would therefore on that account receive less support than the average for the EU; while one producing more of 'other grains' than the average would receive more.

The report on the CAP from Erasmus University, Rotterdam, gives percentages of particular products in total agricultural output for the EU as a whole.[11] The *Annual Abstract of Statistics* allows the calculation of similar figures for Britain.[12] On that basis, British agriculture is biased to the production of cereals, dairy products and meat, all of which are high-subsidy products. These

10   OECD, p. 206
11   Kol and Kuijpers, op. cit., p. 7.
12   AAS, 1996, p. 202

categories account for three-quarters of British farm output, but only slightly more than half of EU output as a whole.

The other half of EU output is 'fruits and vegetables': 16 per cent (Britain 15 per cent); 'wine': 6 per cent (British output not reported); and 'other': 24 per cent (Britain 6 per cent). The OECD does not report on subsidies to the production of fruits and vegetables or wine; and several items in 'other' are heavily subsidised – for example, oilseeds and sugar. It is possible that UK agriculture produces a higher percentage of high-subsidy products than the EU in general, but not, on the basis of these figures, certain. Nevertheless, differences in the composition of farm output between Britain and the rest of the EU may be a source of overestimation in the calculations reported above.

Overall bias

The failure of the OECD figures to include all agricultural products that receive support in the EU is likely to be much the largest source of bias. The estimate above of the costs to Britain of the CAP therefore almost certainly underestimates the true cost.

II EU IMPORT DUTIES

The core issue in assessing how British exports to the EU would be affected by withdrawal is, of course, the level of EU import duties on British goods after withdrawal. But while EU duties are not as formidable as some hold them to be, neither are they as low as others say. The idea that EU tariffs are very low comes from the frequently quoted figure that after the Uruguay Round, the trade-weighted average EU tariff on industrial products is 2.9 per cent. That figure is correct, but it does not mean that Britain would face an EU tariff of only 2.9 per cent were it outside the EU.

Calculating average tariffs

The problem is that the weights used to calculate the 2.9 per cent trade-weighted average tariff are based on the exports to the EU of countries without preferential arrangements with the EU (for example, the US and Japan). To construct this trade-weighted average EU tariff, each individual tariff rate is multiplied by the fraction of total imports into the EU paying that rate. These products for each tariff item are then added together to obtain the trade-weighted average tariff.

To see the difficulty this procedure creates, suppose that non-members without preferential agreements export £99 of good A to the EU, paying duty of 100 per cent and £10,000 of good B, paying duty of 1 per cent. Total trade is £10099. The weight given to the 100 per cent tariff is 99/10099 and the weight given to the 1 per cent tariff is 10000/10099. On that basis, the trade-weighted average EU tariff is less than 2 per cent. But the low weighted-average tariff conceals the possibility – indeed, the near certainty – that the 100 per cent tariff on product A greatly reduces imports of A. The 'low' tariff is consistent with a great deal of EU protection of the A-producing industry in the EU.

In general, a high tariff will reduce imports of the protected good into the EU, reducing the influence of the high tariff on the level of the trade-weighted tariff. In the limit, a completely prohibitive tariff (that is, one that eliminates imports of the protected good) will have no weight at all in the calculation of the trade-weighted tariff. Thus, if the 100 per cent tariff in the example above were raised to 200 per cent, and if this eliminated imports into the EU, the trade-weighted average EU tariff would fall to 1 per cent – the rate on the only remaining imports.

If imports from outside the EU are reduced by high tariffs, however, trade between member-states may be stimulated. The composition of exports to the rest of the EU of insiders, as compared with the exports of outsiders, is likely to be systematically biased towards goods that bear high tariffs if imported from outside the EU. An EU trade-weighted average tariff based on the exports of member-states to one another will therefore probably be higher than one based on exports from outsiders.

Similarly, an EU trade-weighted average tariff based on the current composition of Britain's exports to the rest of the EU is probably more than 2.9 per cent. It is this higher figure, however, that is needed to estimate the effect on British economic welfare of re-imposition of EU duties on British exports to the EU. [13]

How much higher than 2.9 per cent might it be? The EU tariff schedule contains few rates above 20 per cent on industrial goods, but quite a few between 10 and 20 per cent. The highest EU tariffs are on textiles and apparel and related goods. The simple arithmetic average (unweighted) EU tariff on industrial products (HS chapters 25–96) is 5.98 per cent. Removing textiles and apparel (HS chapters 51–64), the unweighted average tariff falls to 5.1 per cent.[14] Six per cent is a better guesstimate than 2.9 per cent of the average EU tariff on current British exports if Britain withdrew

---

13 In principle, such an average tariff should be easy to obtain. It is, though, difficult to obtain the basic data in a form that facilitates electronic manipulation.

14 The figures cited in this paragraph are from J. Michael Finger, Ulrich Reincke and Merlinda Ingco, *The Uruguay Round: statistics on tariff concessions given and received*, Washington DC: The World Bank, 1996.

without any special arrangement regarding trade and tariffs.

A tariff of 6 per cent will reduce trade by more than one of 2.9 per cent, but it is still far from prohibitive. Its effects can be overcome by relatively small adjustments in exchange rates or wage or other costs. Such adjustments would be facilitated by the lower prices of food – and therefore higher real wages – that would follow resignation from the CAP. Repatriations of British contributions to the EU budget would also help.

Dependence of British industries on exports to the EU

The relatively low EU tariff suggests that few EU industries depend upon tariffs for their survival. Nevertheless, as noted above, the EU tariff schedule contains a number of high peaks.

To comment on the likely performance of British industries in international trade after withdrawal from the EU, it is necessary to have some idea of the British tariff that would then apply to imports from the remainder of the EU and the rest of the world. A sensible operating assumption is that the UK adopts the EU tariff, at least initially. Hence, British industries will have the same level of protection against imports from the rest of the world as now, but British tariffs will also be levied on imports from the EU. In addition, of course, British exports to the rest of the EU will face protection. Hence, British industries at risk will be those with a high level of exports to the rest of the EU.

A comparison of British exports to other EU members with exports to non-members gives some idea of how dependent British trade is on EU membership. Table 3 provides some relevant information by SITC (Standard International Trade Classification) industrial divisions.

Column 2 of Table 3 gives exports to the rest of the world as a fraction of exports to the EU. A low number in this column means that the rest of the EU is a more important market than the rest of the world. Ratios less than 0.5, for example, appear in SITC divisions 56 (fertilisers); 57 (plastics in primary forms); 62 (rubber manufactures); 63 (wood and cork manufactures); 75 (office and data processing machines); 78 (road vehicles); and 83 (travel goods).

Only three of these industries, however, make net exports to the EU – divisions 62, 75 and 83. The rest are characterised by net imports from the EU – withdrawal is therefore more likely to improve their position than to worsen it. Of the three with net exports, only one – division 75 – makes large net exports to the rest of the EU. That seems to put it at risk from withdrawal. The industry also has net imports from the rest of the world, however, and these are larger than its net exports to the EU; so EU protection may not be a crucial factor in its survival.

What is remarkable about Table 3 is the broad consistency of performance across industries. More detailed examination might, of course, reveal further problems. The broad picture, though, suggests underlying strength and a lack of dependence on EU tariffs.

III   FOREIGN DIRECT INVESTMENT

The share of foreign direct investment (FDI) into the EU received by Britain is much larger than might be suggested by its share of its EU population or EU GDP. Table 4 summarises the 1998 position.

The US has much the largest share of directly owned foreign capital in the UK. US residents own just short of half of the total,

Table 3 UK exports of industrial products to EU and rest of the world (RoW), 1998, £ million

SITC section and divisions	Exports to EU	Exports to RoW: Exports to EU	Net exports to EU	Net exports to RoW
Section 5: Chemicals and related products				
51. Organic chemicals	2978	0.67	-162	423
52. Inorganic chemicals	703	0.66	108	-13
53. Dyeing, tanning and colouring materials	934	0.66	206	302
54. Medicinal and pharmaceutical products	3116	0.88	702	1740
55. Oils and perfume materials	1483	0.66	199	580
56. Fertilisers	100	0.25	-14	-103
57. Plastics in primary forms	1316	0.41	-740	61
58. Plastics in non-primary forms	894	0.52	-294	139
59. Chemical materials and products n.e.s.	1448	1.00	134	899
Section 5 totals	**12972**	**0.71**	**139**	**4029**
Section 6: Chemicals and related products				
61. Leather, leather manufactures and furskins	153	1.00	25	64
62. Rubber manufactures n.e.s.	1010	0.46	72	-72
63. Wood & cork manufactures	181	0.33	-401	-492
64. Paper and paperboard manufactures	1389	0.58	-2339	-139
65. Textile manufactures	2052	0.60	-946	-791
66. Non-metallic mineral manufactures	2394	0.85	776	-1408
67. Iron and steel	2107	0.59	-315	341
68. Non-ferrous metals	1512	0.62	120	-1511
69. Metal manufactures	2035	0.77	-79	-209
Section 6 totals	**12833**	**0.66**	**-3087**	**-4217**

Section 7: Machinery and transport equipment

71. Power generating machinery and equipment	3814	1.52	1842	1774
72. Machinery for particular industries	2561	1.31	7	1676
73. Metalworking machinery	480	1.37	-65	-23
74. General industrial machinery	3725	0.99	-506	973
75. Office and data processing machines	9344	0.38	2188	-4938
76. Telecom and sound-recording equipment	6137	0.54	2614	-1423
77. Electrical machinery and apparatus	6991	0.66	1048	-2997
78. Road vehicles	10266	0.44	-8951	579
79. Other transport equipment	2196	1.73	937	-1106
Section 7 totals	**45514**	**0.73**	**-884**	**-5486**

Section 8: Miscellaneous manufactured articles

81. Prefabricated buildings	284	0.71	249	-12
82. Furniture and parts thereof	586	0.68	507	-255
83. Travel goods	104	0.44	95	-380
84. Articles of apparel	1973	0.51	1793	-3735
85. Footwear	270	1.01	205	-504
87. Scientific instruments	2148	1.33	2016	469
88. Photographic equipment	1011	0.79	941	-522
89. Miscellaneous manufactured articles n.e.s.	4121	1.16	3801	-1697
Section 8 totals	**10495**	**0.99**	**9605**	**-6639**
SECTION 5 TO 8 TOTALS	**81814**	**0.75**	**5773**	**-12313**

Source: *Overseas Trade Statistics of the UK, December 1998*.
Note: n.e.s. = not elsewhere specified.
  SITC = Standard International Trade Classification.
  Sums may not equal totals due to rounding.

Table 4 **National ownership of directly owned foreign capital in the UK, book values, 1998, £ million**

EU	48,789
Of which:	
France	13,440
Germany	10,218
Netherlands	14,208
Switzerland	15,137
USA	90,341
Australia	5,877
Japan	6,624
Other Asia	2,665
Total	183,544

Source: Office of National Statistics, Overseas Direct Investment 1998, pp. 75–6.

more than their 41 per cent share in 1994. Japanese companies hold about 3.5 per cent of the total stock of directly owned foreign capital in Britain.

For US and EU investors, the decision to invest in Britain is primarily economic. As the earlier discussion of EU tariffs suggests, EU tariffs are not so fearsome that their imposition on exports from Britain to the EU would eliminate Britain from consideration as a site for investments.

Some inward FDI, however, may have an essentially political purpose. The exports to the EU of Japanese and Korean companies, in particular, were battered by EU anti-dumping actions in the late 1980s and early 1990s. Companies from those countries have probably decided that the best way to protect themselves against such EU actions is by producing in the EU rather than exporting finished products to it. British withdrawal from the EU might have a substantial effect on such 'political' investments – location in Britain would no longer buy political approval from Brussels.

Impact of FDI on the British economy

The British government pays for FDI, and this is a major reason for caution when assessing the benefits that FDI brings. Payments are both direct and indirect.

Direct payment

The comment of the *Financial Times* (10 July 1996) was noted in Chapter 4: 'Even for large schemes creating many jobs, few companies secure more than £20,000 a post.' That is a substantial subsidy. Probably the figure is now out of date, and probably the current figure is higher: as also noted in Chapter 4, £30,000 a job seems to have been offered to Nissan in 2001. Publicly available statistics, however, are insufficient to allow calculation.

Indirect payment

FDI, especially from Japan, may be a response to EU protection, real or imagined. That raises the possibility that companies will invest in the EU even if it is more expensive to produce in the EU than to export to it from elsewhere.

A duty of 25 per cent on widget imports into the EU, for example, may cause a Japanese widget producer to decide to produce widgets in the EU, even though its EU costs of production are up to 25 per cent higher than its costs of production in Japan. But servicing the EU market from production in the EU, rather than from production in Japan, means that imports from Japan cease, and, therefore, revenue from duties on imports ceases also. EU widget buyers may pay less for widgets, but the EU as a whole is still worse off. In effect, the tariff revenue has been paid to the

Japanese company as a *quid pro quo* for locating production in the EU and for the higher costs of production that relocation entails.

FDI and British welfare

Payments for FDI, whether direct or indirect, raise the possibility that FDI makes the payer worse off. Members of the British economy benefit from FDI when British factors of production receive higher returns than they otherwise would, which might come about either because of an increased demand for their services, or as a consequence of positive externalities generated by the investments. They may also gain as a consequence of British taxation on the profits from the investment of foreign residents. Returns from these sources, however, may be entirely dissipated by direct and indirect payments to inward investors.

IV INTERNATIONAL TRANSACTIONS IN SERVICES

A principal difference between industries producing goods and industries providing services is that service industries are not usually protected by tariffs or quotas. The 'invisible' properties of services – the fact that customs officers often cannot detect them as they cross frontiers – mean that many service industries *cannot* be protected by border measures.

A second characteristic of services, however, is that cross-border trade is itself often either infeasible, or not the preferred means of providing a service. Service transactions often require the provider and the receiver of the service to be in geographical proximity with one another. International transactions in services are therefore more likely to require some form of international factor movement than international transactions in goods. Bans or restrictions on presence and establishment are effective barriers to international transactions in the service sector – in many service industries, from a protectionist point of view, a more than adequate substitute for tariffs.

Restrictions on presence and establishment, however, are only part of the more general problem for international transactions in services that is raised by regulation of service industries – fiduciary regulation, occupational licensing and so on. Whatever the intrinsic merits of such regulation, it is a primary means of protecting domestic providers of services from foreign competition. Laws, administrative actions and regulations often bear with a particularly heavy weight on foreign providers of services.

The problems of policy that arise from these differences between goods and services were at the heart of the single-market programme. To cut short a long story, Article 49 of the Treaty of European Union (formerly Article 59) calls for free trade in services within the EU. Nevertheless, for many services, movement from the 1957 starting line defined by the Treaty of Rome was by the mid-1980s close to imperceptible. That was not true for any manufacturing industry. As a consequence, the bulk of the single-market programme set out in the mid-1980s was in fact concerned with liberalisation of trade in services between the member-states.

The single-market solution to liberalising trade in services derives from the principle of 'mutual recognition' of standards that was developed for trade in goods. The thrust of the programme was to negotiate minimum standards for regulating the provision of a service and then, provided that the regulations of a member-state satisfy those standards, to allow service providers from that member-state freedom of transaction within the single market.

An important element of this freedom is the principle of home-country control. Provided that the minimum regulatory standard is met, a service provider from one member-state is legally free to establish in another member-state but will be regulated by the authorities of its *home* country. A British building society, for example, should in principle be able to open branches in Spain which will be subject to British, not Spanish, regulatory control.

Since rights of establishment are at the heart of the issue, one further element of EU law calls for comment. This is Article 48 of the Treaty of European Union (formerly Article 58) in the chapter dealing with the right of establishment, which says, in its entirety:

> Companies or firms formed in accordance with the law of a Member State and having their registered office, central administration or principal place of business within the Community shall, for the purposes of this Chapter, be treated in the same way as natural persons who are nationals of Member States.
>
> 'Companies or firms' means companies or firms constituted under civil or commercial law, including co-operative societies, and other legal persons governed by public or private law, save for those which are non-profit making.

A US service-providing company can therefore establish a subsidiary in, say, the Netherlands. It can then sell services throughout the EU, under the regulatory control, in principle, of the Dutch authorities.

Costs and benefits of withdrawal

The discussion above should make it clear that a great deal of information is needed to attempt to make a monetary estimate of the costs or benefits of withdrawal for trade in services. Such an estimate is not feasible in this study – nor probably in any other. Nevertheless, some propositions about the costs and benefits of withdrawal can be made, one of which is that in the worst possible case, the costs cannot be high, relative to GDP.

Cross-border trade

As noted in Table 1 on p. 76, cross-border exports of services to other member states amount to 2.5 per cent of GDP. Moreover, the services that are exported across borders by the UK – maritime transport, travel, financial services, royalties, consultancy, professional services – are not typically subject to EU regulatory barriers to trade (although some important areas are subject to single-market harmonisation measures). In other sectors where such regulatory barriers exist, or arguably or potentially exist, such as civil aviation, international treaties provide minimum levels of treatment of one state by another – in the case of civil aviation, for example, by the Chicago Convention of 1944. The presence in the EU of US service providers in almost all of the areas noted above is irrefutable evidence that EU membership is not necessary for successful provision of these services in the EU.

Establishment trade

The position of US companies in the single market defines the worst case for UK companies that provide services in the EU through local presence in other member-states of the EU. A

British-owned company that provides services through establishment in another member-state, and is subject to regulation by the authorities of that state, will be in exactly the same situation if Britain withdraws from the EU. But a company that now provides services through establishments regulated by the British authorities may find, if Britain is no longer a member of the EU, that it has to choose a new EU 'home' – which is effectively also a choice of regulatory authority.

Clearly, this may create inconvenience: for example, learning to operate under new regulations and accommodating new and possibly less sympathetic regulatory authorities. The effect of such problems on sales, however, is open to doubt – regulations and regulatory authorities change all the time, and service providers constantly adjust to those changes.

APPENDIX B
THE BASIS OF COMPARISON:
THE WORLD TRADING SYSTEM

Introduction

Any assessment of the benefits and costs of the UK's membership of the European Union must have a baseline against which those costs and benefits can be measured. The obvious baseline to choose for that purpose is the position the UK would be in if it were an independent member of the world trading system, free of any trade blocs or special trade arrangements.

It is not necessarily realistic to suppose that the UK would find itself in such a position if it were for any reason to cease its membership of the European Union. It is more realistic to suppose that in such a situation the UK would develop special trading relationships, possibly including some form of special relationship with the European Union itself. Before the UK joined the Common Market in 1973, it was a member of the European Free Trade Area (EFTA) and enjoyed special Commonwealth trading links.

Independent membership of the world trading system *simpliciter* is therefore probably very much a 'worst case' scenario, rather than a 'best available alternative' to membership of the European Union. Chapter 3 considered some alternative policy options which might be available to the UK, and sought to compare them with that baseline scenario.

The Uruguay Round, GATT 1994 and the Marrakesh Agreement

The baseline entails consideration of the world trading system as it now exists after completion of the Uruguay Round of negotiations conducted under the auspices of the General Agreement on Tariffs and Trade (GATT). These negotiations led in April 1994 to the conclusion of the Marrakesh Agreement establishing the World Trade Organization, together with a substantially revised GATT (GATT 1994) and a series of related multilateral agreements, including the General Agreement on Trade in Services (GATS). Those agreements cover the great bulk of economically significant world trading nations.

The present-day multilateral world trade system is very different from the environment which existed in 1972 when Britain took its decision to join the then Common Market. Under the auspices of GATT, great strides have been taken in reducing the levels of tariffs and the impact of quotas, and in making inroads into non-tariff barriers of various kinds. The 1994 Marrakesh Agreement substantially improved the effectiveness of the remedies available against a wide range of protectionist measures and trade practices.

The cornerstone of the international trading system is the principle of non-discrimination, under which trading nations should not impose discriminatory barriers against particular trading partners.[1] As far as customs measures are concerned, they must accord to all trading partners the same treatment as is accorded to 'most favoured nations'. The exception to this principle is that countries may become members of free trade areas or cus-

---

1   GATT 1994, Articles I and III.

toms unions, in which case they are entitled to impose zero tariffs on trade within the free trade area or customs union.[2] The European Community itself is a customs union permitted under this provision of GATT. A second aspect of the obligation not to discriminate arises in relation to internal measures, where it is required that members impose the same standards on imported goods as on goods of their own national origin.[3] The general rule under GATT 1994 is that 'quantitative restrictions' on imports and exports (quotas or import bans) are prohibited.[4]

Apart from the 1994 GATT agreement itself, the Uruguay Round negotiations concluded a number of highly technical but important 'multilateral agreements' which have the effect of reducing barriers to trade. These include agreements on customs valuations, fees and formalities, marks of origin, and import licensing procedures. An Agreement on the Application of Sanitary and Phytosanitary Measures (measures for the protection of human, animal or plant health) requires that any such measures which affect trade are to be based on scientific principles, and must not be arbitrary or discriminatory. An Agreement on Technical Barriers to Trade applies similar principles of non-discrimination and necessity based on scientific requirements to technical standards which trading countries impose on goods; it contains a procedural code for the formulation and adoption of such standards.

---

2   GATT 1994, Article XXIV.

3   GATT 1994, Article III.

4   GATT 1994, Article XI. It is, however, important to note that special rules apply to the agricultural sector and to textiles, and in these areas the general rules of GATT are greatly weakened. There is also an important exception to the general rule in the case of cinema films, where quotas are allowed – a measure insisted on by France.

The Agreement on Subsidies and Countervailing Measures prohibits certain state subsidies which are contingent on export performance, or which are conditional on the use of domestic goods in place of imported goods. Other forms of state subsidy which have the effect of benefiting exporters, or deterring importers of competing goods, although not prohibited, are defined as 'actionable'. 'Actionable' subsidies give rise to a right on the part of other affected countries to take counter-measures.

Before the Marrakesh Agreement, the agricultural sector effectively escaped international regulation under the GATT. That is probably the sector where tariffs, quotas, export subsidies and other forms of governmental intervention which massively distort international trade have been most rife: the Common Agricultural Policy of the EEC is a major example. The Agreement on Agriculture concluded during the Uruguay Round has the stated aim of seeking to reduce barriers to trade in that sector; to secure the progressive reduction in government support for domestic producers; and to establish a fair system of export competition. It is clear that there is much further to go in the agricultural sector in securing a liberal world trading régime: there are severe political problems in many countries in reducing protectionism in this field.

GATS for the first time provides for a multilateral framework for the promotion of free trade in the field of services. At present it consists of a series of general principles rather than specific obligations: a more ambitious attempt to liberalise trade in the field of services was sabotaged by a number of parties, including the EC largely at French instigation. Nonetheless, it lays down the basic structure on which a more ambitious system may be expected to develop in future. It covers the supply of services by cross-border provision; by the supply of services to visitors from other countries; and through a commercial presence or the presence of representatives in the territory of another state. In services, the most favoured nation principle is to be observed, and discriminatory measures in, for example, the recognition of qualifications are banned.

Disputes settlement under the WTO regime

Apart from the substantive agreements which have been outlined above, probably the most significant consequence of the Marrakesh Agreement was the strengthening of measures to ensure compliance with free-trading obligations. Marrakesh established a new body, the World Trade Organization (WTO), which has supervisory and arbitral functions.[5] The so-called Trade Policy Review Mechanism involves the periodic review by the WTO's secretariat of the trade policies and trade-related measures of member-states, including those of customs unions such as the EC. Far more important, the Marrakesh Agreement has effectively removed the veto right which had previously hamstrung the GATT disputes procedure.

There is now a general right for member-states to invoke the disputes procedure in the event of a perceived breach by any other member of the 1994 GATT Agreement or of any of the associated multilateral agreements (outlined above) which were concluded in the Uruguay Round.[6] In some circumstances the procedure can be

---

5   Functions of the WTO are set out in the Marrakesh Agreement, Article III.
6   Understanding on Rules and Procedures Governing the Settlement of Disputes, Article I(1). The Understanding sets out the disputes procedures.

invoked in the absence of an actual breach, if the actions of one member adversely affect the trading interests of another member.[7] The WTO appoints a three- or five-member disputes panel to rule on the complaint[8] and either party can appeal to a Standing Appellate Body.[9]

Rulings of disputes panels are ultimately enforceable through the authorisation of retaliatory measures.[10] These measures should initially relate to the same sector as that in which the violation occurred, but if such retaliation is not likely to be effective, then retaliation may be authorised under other aspects of the same agreement; if that is not effective then, if circumstances are serious enough, the complaining party may seek authorisation to retaliate under one of the other Uruguay Round agreements.

The purpose of these measures is to try to ensure that the past danger of uncontrolled escalation of trade disputes into trade wars is avoided; at the same time, countries which suffer an unjustified interference with their rights under GATT and the related agreements are entitled to take proportionate measures to punish the defaulting party and to protect their own trade. There was reason to fear that the division of the world into trading blocs could lead to an increasing breakdown of the multilateral world trading system outside and between those blocs. As it is, it seems that the con-

---

7   GATT 1994, Article XXIII(1)(a) provides for so-called 'violation complaints', whilst XXIII(1)(b) and (c) provide for complaints to be brought in the absence of violations where there is nullification or impairment to the complaining party of the benefits accruing to it under the agreements.

8   Understanding, Article 8(5).

9   Understanding, Article 17. This is a seven-member body, which sits in panels of three to hear appeals.

10 Understanding, Article 22(2).

clusion of the Uruguay Round at Marrakesh has maintained progress towards liberalisation of general world trade in important respects.

Thus, the trading environment which the UK would face on our baseline case is not one where it would be shut out from trading with other countries, including the EC itself. Clearly, the world trading system is less well developed than the internal market within the EC. It must therefore be asked in what ways and to what extent the UK's position would differ as regards the access of its exports to the single market if it were to be outside the EC, relying on access for its exports on GATT 1994 and its associated agreements. This issue is addressed in Chapters 2 and 4.

Relationship between the EC and GATT

The relationship between the European Community and GATT is complex, since both the Community and the original member-states are members of GATT 1994. Responsibility for the EC's external commercial policy is a matter of Community competence and is discharged by the European Commission subject to the oversight of the Council of Ministers.[11] However, many aspects of GATT 1994 and its related agreements go beyond customs matters and impinge on internal measures which may produce effects on international trade. For this reason, the European Court has ruled that although the aspects of the Uruguay Round agreement relating to trade in goods are within the exclusive competence of the Community, the conclusion of the Uruguay Round agreements as

---

11 Treaty of Rome, Article 133.

a whole was a matter of joint competence between the Community and the member-states.[12]

EC member-states are individual signatories of the Uruguay Round agreements, and have assumed individual responsibility at the international level for the discharge of the obligations assumed by them under the agreements, whether or not those obligations fall within the scope of the Community's competence.[13] Under Community rules, the member-states must act jointly in the WTO forum,[14] and the European Commission has responsibility for maintaining relations with the WTO.[15] However, these arrangements mean that at an international level the UK would continue to enjoy its status as a member-state of the WTO were it to cease to belong to the EC, but would of course cease to be subject to the internal EC requirements in that forum of joint action and representation by the European Commission.

The strengthening of multilateral free-trade rules under the Uruguay Round has led to a novel situation for the EC. Its institutions have been used to being in the position of exercising supervision or control over the activities of the member-states where measures taken by member-states conflict with the EC's common-market or single-market rules. Now the EC itself is in a position where its own rules are subject to review under the auspices of the WTO, and can be found in breach of international obligations by GATT disputes panels. International agreements between the

---

12   *Re the Uruguay Round Treaties*, Opinion 1/94, [1995] 1 CMLR 205. The Treaty of Nice will amend Article 133 and expand the scope of the EC's common commercial policy to cover services and other trade-related fields of policy.

13   Understanding on Interpretation of Article XXIV of GATT 1994.

14   Treaty of Maastricht, Article 19(1).

15   Treaty of Rome, Article 302.

Community and non-member countries can potentially be legally binding and directly applicable within the EC's own legal order;[16] however, the ECJ has declined to give direct effect to provisions of the GATT to quash a Community regulation found to be inconsistent with GATT by a disputes panel.[17] The ECJ's selective application of the rule of law when it comes to international obligations assumed by the EC forms an interesting contrast with its insistence that all member-states are subject to the supremacy of Community law. It remains to be seen whether the more effective enforcement mechanisms under the Uruguay Round will over time lead to a change of heart in the attitude of the EC institutions towards compliance with the EC's multilateral trade obligations.[18]

---

16 Case 48/74: *Charmasson v. Minister of Economic Affairs* [1975] 2 CMLR 208.

17 Case C-280/93: *Re Banana Agreements: Germany v. EC Council* [1993] ECR I-3367.

18 For a criticism of the *Bananas* decision, see Petersmann, 'The GATT Dispute Settlement System as an Instrument of the Foreign Trade Policy of the EC', in O'Keefe and Emiliou (eds.), *The European Union and World Trade Law*, 1996.

ABOUT THE IEA

The Institute is a research and educational charity (No. CC 235 351), limited by guarantee. Its mission is to improve understanding of the fundamental institutions of a free society with particular reference to the role of markets in solving economic and social problems.

The IEA achieves its mission by:

- a high quality publishing programme
- conferences, seminars, lectures and other events
- outreach to school and college students
- brokering media introductions and appearances

The IEA, which was established in 1955 by the late Sir Antony Fisher, is an educational charity, not a political organisation. It is independent of any political party or group and does not carry on activities intended to affect support for any political party or candidate in any election or referendum, or at any other time. It is financed by sales of publications, conference fees and voluntary donations.

In addition to its main series of publications the IEA also publishes a quarterly journal, *Economic Affairs*, and has two specialist programmes – Environment and Technology, and Education.

The IEA is aided in its work by a distinguished international Academic Advisory Council and an eminent panel of Honorary Fellows. Together with other academics, they review prospective IEA publications, their comments being passed on anonymously to authors. All IEA papers are therefore subject to the same rigorous independent refereeing process as used by leading academic journals.

IEA publications enjoy widespread classroom use and course adoptions in schools and universities. They are also sold throughout the world and often translated/reprinted.

Since 1974 the IEA has helped to create a world-wide network of 100 similar institutions in over 70 countries. They are all independent but share the IEA's mission.

Views expressed in the IEA's publications are those of the authors, not those of the Institute (which has no corporate view), its Managing Trustees, Academic Advisory Council members or senior staff.

Members of the Institute's Academic Advisory Council, Honorary Fellows, Trustees and Staff are listed on the following page.

The Institute gratefully acknowledges financial support for its publications programme and other work from a generous benefaction by the late Alec and Beryl Warren.

The Institute of Economic Affairs
2 Lord North Street, Westminster, London SW1P 3LB
Tel: 020 7799 8900
Fax: 020 7799 2137
Email: iea@iea.org.uk
Internet: iea.org.uk

129

For information about subscriptions to IEA publications, please contact:

Subscriptions
The Institute of Economic Affairs
2 Lord North Street
London SW1P 3LB

Tel: 020 7799 8900
Fax: 020 7799 2137
Website: www.iea.org.uk/books/subscribe.htm

Other papers recently published by the IEA include:

WHO, What and Why?

Transnational Government, Legitimacy and the World Health Organization
Roger Scruton
Occasional Paper 113
ISBN 0 255 36487 3

The World Turned Rightside Up

A New Trading Agenda for the Age of Globalisation
John C. Hulsman
Occasional Paper 114
ISBN 0 255 36495 4

The Representation of Business in English Literature

Introduced and edited by Arthur Pollard
Readings 53
ISBN 0 255 36491 1

Anti-Liberalism 2000

The Rise of New Millennium Collectivism
David Henderson
Occasional Paper 115
ISBN 0 255 36497 0

Waging the War of Ideas
John Blundell
Occasional Paper 119
ISBN 0 255 36500 4

To order copies of currently available IEA papers, or to enquire about availability, please contact:

Lavis Marketing
73 Lime Walk
Oxford OX3 7AD

Tel: 01865 767575
Fax: 01865 750079
Email: orders@lavismarketing.co.uk